P. W. H. Cochrane
July 1991.

EIGHT DAYS A WEEK

Diary of a Professional Cricketer

JONATHAN AGNEW

The inside story of the 1988 season

RINGPRESS

First published in 1988 by
Ringpress Books
an imprint of Ringpress Limited,
Spirella House, Letchworth, Herts SG6 4ET

Text © 1988 Jonathan Agnew and Ringpress Limited

ISBN 0 948955 30 9

Typeset by DP Photosetting, Aylesbury, Bucks
Production Consultants: Landmark Ltd of London
Printed and bound in Great Britain by The Bath Press

Contents

To my wife Bev and daughter Jennifer.
Thanks for putting up with me during a difficult summer.
And to the final delivery of the season ...
our second daughter, Rebecca, born on Sunday, September 18.

Acknowledgements

To Dad, for getting me started.

Les Berry and Maurice Hallam, for their help and encouragement, and Mike Turner, for taking a chance on me.

Geoff Blackburn, for all the facts and figures contained in this book.

Graham Morris, David Munden, and the *Leicester Mercury* for their photographs.

And, above all, to the lads on the professional circuit, a big thank you for all the pleasure and pain which makes a cricket season.

Foreword

By MARTIN JOHNSON

of *The Independent*

It first became apparent to me that Jon Agnew had a way with words shortly after describing his bowling in a match at Edgbaston as belonging to the primary school playground variety. The phone rang at home and my wife, detecting nothing other than his usual cheery demeanour, said: "It's Aggie. Wants to know if you've got a minute."

"Morning Aggers," I said. "What can I do for you?" Around five minutes later, when Hurricane Agnew had blown itself out, I got my first words in. "What you want me to do with my typewriter is, I suspect, a physical impossibility. However, I have scarcely had my shortcomings in the art of cricket appreciation described with such eloquence. Have you considered a career in journalism?" And with that, he decided to abandon plans for winter employment as Fred Trueman's pipe cleaner, joined Radio Leicester as a sports reporter instead, and now I find I can't even have a decent chinwag with him in the bar after the game. "Sorry, can't stop. Off to my room with the old word processor. You know what these deadlines are."

He was a stringy 18 year old fresh out of Uppingham School, and it took him precisely four deliveries in county cricket to prove that he could knock over Test players, as well as sixth formers, with his raw pace. David Lloyd's off stump flew so far back it almost impaled Roger Tolchard, the Leicestershire wicketkeeper. "Hello," we thought, "what have we got here?" Within a month he had won a Whitbread Scholarship to Australia, and more headlines followed there. Invited into an England net in Melbourne, he promptly crusted the captain, Mike Brearley. It would have been better had he been able to serve his apprenticeship without so much national expectation, making steady rather than spectacular progress while hopefully developing a frame that at 18 made it look as though you were viewing a Lowry through one of those elongated funfair mirrors.

We waited for him to fill out, and we're still waiting. The first time I met his father Philip, I knew he never would. A chip (or rather a crisp) off the old block. At dinner, which is normally his fifth or sixth cooked meal of the day, you can barely see him over the top of the plate. His first injury for Leicestershire was a pulled muscle, which was a relief. No-one knew he had a muscle up until then.

He is still thought of as injury prone, which is unfair. Initially, it is true, the Grace Road air would reverberate to the gentle thwack of leather on willow, and the twang of an Agnew hamstring. Small boys queued up to swap their Bradman autographs for something far more valuable. A signed scorecard with both Agnew and Les Taylor on it. For many years now he has been one of the fittest members on the Grace Road staff, and if he is carrying anything, it is an injured look when people like Peter May suggest otherwise. He even got through this book without having to call in the physio, which is not quite as daft as it sounds. Derek Pringle once ricked his back writing a letter.

I don't think he will mind me saying, though, at the risk of another phone call, that the maturing process took rather longer with him than some. The county cricket circuit is the hardest in the world, the only full-time professional road show, and if you had suggested to one or two old sweats in the dressing room circa the late Seventies that Agnew was searching for a book title, *8 hours a week* might well have topped the poll. "Gin and tonic cricketer" was perhaps a little over the top, but when the going got tough, Aggie rarely got going.

Without perhaps knowing it, he provided me with much pleasure in his early years by his deportment in the field, which was clearly not his natural habitat. Whenever he signalled to the dressing room, I fancied he was calling for a deckchair and a Pimms, and the twelfth man would hang on to the pain killing spray like a baton in a relay race. Occasionally (and more often than not while engaged in what ought to have been a routine piece of fielding) the ball would pass through his hands and make contact with some part of his anatomy. In John Wayne films, the relevant phrase was "it's only a scratch." In Agnew cameos, it was "I think it's probably fatal. Send for the priest."

Agnew is not, by nature, aggressive, in the way that one of his mentors, Ken Higgs, certainly was. If someone snicked Higgs over the slips, a pretty one-sided conversation would ensue. When Viv Richards did it to Agnew at Taunton one afternoon, he decided to venture a tentative "that was bit lucky old chap." Viv duly gave him a volley, which resulted in Agnew wandering off to mid-on with one of his bewildered looks. "He called me a turkey. What's a turkey?"

In his case, something that would provide Christmas dinner for one, provided they'd had a filling starter. However, whenever Agnew comes out to bat, he manages to make Cyril Smith look anorexic, such is the volume of padding underneath his sweater. In one innings at Chesterfield, he kept smashing Michael Holding through the covers. Michael, not best pleased, then began producing the "let's see you hit that one for four, then" ball, with the result that the game ended up being played at least four pitches away from the one the groundsman had originally designated. In the end, and I kid you not, it was the first and only time I've ever seen the square leg umpire duck beneath a bouncer.

Provided the ball is pitched well up, Agnew can be a spectacular striker of the ball, as he showed at Scarborough towards the end of the 1987 season. Having gone in as nightwatchman, he was well on the way towards a career best 90 from 68 balls (including six sixes) when his captain Peter Willey walked in. He could not resist it. "Now then, Will" he said, "just look for the ones and give me the strike. I'm in a bit of nick out here, you know."

Agnew has a wide repertoire of strokes in the dressing room banter and repartee stakes as well, his skills honed in a constant head-to-head with Les Taylor, one of the most natural funny men in county cricket. As is often the case with people of widely differing backgrounds, they have a great rapport.

Early in the season that is the subject of this book, Agnew was seriously considering leaving the game to take up an offer with Radio Leicester as their sports programme producer. It was a difficult decision, particularly with a young family to think about, but in the end he decided that he had a lot more to offer the game. So he does, but I'm sure he will ultimately end up in some form of sports journalism. I know from listening to him (and talking to him, on occasions) on the radio, and reading his various scribblings, that he has a natural aptitude for the job. If and when it ever brings him into a cricketing press box, he will be a more than welcome addition to it.

ALL WIRED UP: Agnew the broadcaster.

David Munden

Introduction

One wet and windy night in February 1988, Peter Baxter interviewed me for Test Match Special on BBC Radio. He played it during the lunch break of a day's play in the Second Test in New Zealand. The subject was the recent announcement that I was to retire from first class cricket. It had been a very difficult decision. The previous season had been easily the most successful of my ten-year career. I had taken over one hundred first class wickets. But I was overlooked for a place on England's winter tours, which disappointed me deeply.

I spent the winter working as the sports producer for BBC Radio Leicester, which meant being solely responsible for the station's coverage of sport. I fell in love with the job. It was so different, and I had become disillusioned with cricket. I believed my best chance of playing for England again had gone. Then I was told that the sports producer's position would have to be filled permanently. I was caught in a terrible dilemma. If I got the job, which is very rarely vacated, I would have to retire from first class cricket in September. I would have just one season left.

I was 28 years old with a family to support, and unless you are a regular England player, there is no financial security in professional cricket. Winter employment is extremely hard to find. I felt that I was not being responsible by simply plodding on from one cricket season to the next.

I applied for the job, and got it. But the news of my appointment was leaked, and I found myself caught in the middle as the inevitable media interest grew. On the one hand I was defending my decision to retire. On the other I was trying desperately to ensure that my bridges would not be burned as far as my England ambitions were concerned.

On that same wet and windy night John Sellers, a publisher by trade, and also a cricket nut, was listening to Test Match Special on Radio Three. He heard the interview, and the seeds for the book were immediately sown.

Situations alter, and my change of heart has been well publicised. However, when I started to write this book I was convinced that I was recording the events of my last season as a professional cricketer.

Jonathan Agnew

ALL FIRED UP: Agnew the bowler.

Graham Morris

The Cast

David Gower
Left hand batsman.
Nickname: Lubo
The skipper. One of the most recognisable sportsmen in the world, but
success has not changed him at all.
Often criticised for his laid back
approach to cricket and life in
general, he believes professional
sportsmen should be able to motivate themselves rather than have
someone standing over them crack-
ing the whip. Loves winter sports,
particularly bobsled, and has gone
solo down the famous Cresta Run.
Has been known to enjoy a glass of
red wine as long as it is vintage, and
worth not less than £150 a bottle.

Leicester Mercury

7

Nigel Briers

Right hand opening batsman
Nickname: Kudu (after African antelope of that name which is instantly recognisable by its larger-than-average ears)
Leicestershire born and bred, playing for the county means an awful lot to Nigel. Appointed vice-captain at the start of the season, he will lead the side when Gower is away on Test duty. Mainly a front foot player, he has recently taken up opening the innings. Renowned as a battler.

Leicester Mercury

Justin Benson

Right hand batsman.
Nickname: Rambo
Second year on the playing staff, aggressive batsman and excellent out-fielder. Dress sense makes Michael Foot look smart.

Leicester Mercury

Tim Boon

Right hand opening batsman
Nickname: Codeye (Do not ask me why!)
Easily the unluckiest first class cricketer in the world. Whenever a ball hits him it breaks a bone. He missed an entire season with a broken leg sustained in a car crash in South Africa. One of the most natural players in the side, has adapted to opening the batting for the sake of the team rather than out of personal preference. His house

Leicester Mercury

8

has become a home for stray cricketers, with several members of the second team lodging there.

Russell Cobb
Right hand opening batsman.
Nickname: Cobby
Better three-day player than one-day player, so has never been a settled member of the team. No-one has worked harder at his game; he is always to be found within twenty yards of a net. Gutsy player of fast bowling.

Leicester Mercury

Philip De Freitas
Right hand bat. Fast bowler
Nickname: Daffy
Incredibly talented all-round cricketer in the Ian Botham mould. Capable of changing the course of a match within a few minutes. Extremely competitive character. Interesting dress sense with greens and purples the "in" colours at the moment.

Leicester Mercury

George Ferris
Right hand bat. Fast bowler
Nickname: Slug (Vulg.)
Our Antiguan overseas player. Protege of Andy Roberts. Mean and vicious on the field, extremely gentle and comical off it. Relishes the opportunity to show off his batting skills, and can hit the ball a long way. Usually does not, however.

Leicester Mercury

9

Peter Hepworth
Right hand batsman.
Nickname: Heppers
Second year on the playing staff. Family friend of Geoff Boycott, who advised him to come to Leicester rather than Yorkshire. Plenty of talent. Will be looking to take Gower's place during Test matches.

Leicester Mercury

Chris Lewis
Right hand bat. Fast bowler
Nickname: Luigi
Extremely talented all rounder. Bowls fast off only a short run up. Brilliant fielder. Slightly less eccentric dress sense than Daffy, but only just.

Leicester Mercury

Laurie Potter
Right hand bat. Left-arm spinner
Nickname: Pottsy
Recently signed from Kent, he still retains strong Australian accent. Has hands like buckets, so is always to be found at first slip. Barely recognisable from a couple of years ago following radical diet. Slimmed right down to 14 stone.

Leicester Mercury

10

Peter Such
Right hand bat (just) Off spinner
Nickname: Suchy
Recent acquisition from Notts. Only spinner I know who bowls in deep sea diving boots. His batting just prevents him from being classed as a genuine all-rounder. He does tell a story, though, of when he smashed Malcolm Marshall for four through third man.

Leicester Mercury

Les Taylor
Right hand bat. Fast bowler
Nickname: Spud
My biggest mate in the game, although the casual onlooker would never believe it. Les is deaf in one ear, which leads to enormous problems on the field with the captain having to bellow himself hoarse to get his attention at third man. Extraordinary batsman famous for the Shilton Drive, which he perfected without the aid of a coaching manual. Has been known to reduce opposing bowlers to nervous wrecks if he gets into double figures.

Leicester Mercury

Lloyd Tennant
Right hand bat. Seam bowler
Nickname: does not have one (yet).
Apprentice fast bowler in the Higgs mould. Bowls at least three thousand overs per year in the nets.

Leicester Mercury

11

James Whitaker
Right hand batsman
Nickname: Jimmy

My old school mate. We have been playing for the same team for thirteen years. Explosive and unorthodox batsman, regularly employing a self-taught short arm jab. Closely resembles a lame dromedary when in full flight in the outfield.

Leicester Mercury

Philip Whitticase
Right hand bat. Wicketkeeper.
Nicknames: Roddy/Roland Rat. (His kit bag resembles a rat's nest in both physical appearance and odour.)

Our stumper, Phil is excellent in the role of team motivator when in the field. My regular travelling companion, and easily the worst navigator in the club. Has slightly unusual taste in music, favouring the likes of The Goblins and The Hoppers (I think).

Leicester Mercury

Peter Willey
Right hand batsman. Off spinner.
Nickname: Will.

Team's senior statesman. Beneath tough northern exterior lies a boyish sense of humour. Apparently. Known for his outstanding bravery, for which he is rewarded with regular trips to the West Indies. Has ability to detect approaching rain from a range of three hundred miles.

Leicester Mercury

Ken Higgs
Leicestershire county coach
Nickname: Higgy
One of the all time great seam bowlers. He still swings it away in the nets, largely because his ball has been doctored with Mr Sheen. No-one has ever scored a run off Higgy, and he despairs when we bowl loosely. Famous for friendly words of advice such as: "If you don't get eight wickets out there today, you'll be down the dole office."

Leicester Mercury

Craig Mortimer
Leicestershire Physiotherapist
Craig has the best of modern equipment at his disposal but has been known to threaten acupuncture on stubborn injuries. As a result he boasts an amazing recovery rate. The sight of L. B. Taylor opening his door sends him into an unusual spasm.

Leicester Mercury

Mike Turner
Chief Executive
Nickname: Sir.
The boss!

Leicester Mercury

13

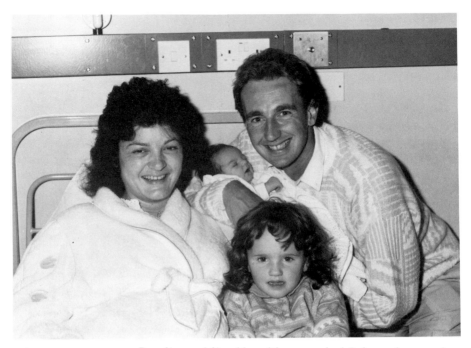

THE FAMILY AGNEW: Bev, Jon and Jennifer with new arrival Rebecca, born on the last day of the 1988 first class season. David Munden

CHAPTER ONE

Back to Work

23 March

JONATHAN AGNEW. England cricketer? County cricketer? Or former cricketer ... After everything that had been said and done during the winter, I felt real excitement as I drove into Grace Road this morning. The first day of any new season provokes nervous anticipation. But I surprised myself. There had been so much talk of my retirement over the past few weeks, that I had been beginning to dread the first day back. I was unsure what the reaction of the lads would be, but I had no need to worry. I bumped into my old sparring partner Les Taylor in the car park, and he reckoned that it was an original way to make sure that I was selected. "I'm going to threaten them with going back down the pit."

Les has been my closest friend at Leicestershire for years. Ever since he lent me his spare pair of boots at the start of my first match for the county second eleven. I had left mine behind at school! I lugged my kit bag up to the first team dressing room, and sat down in my usual spot: crammed up in the corner I had inherited from Ken Higgs. It always has the revolting smell of jockstraps and batting gloves wafting from the drying machine. I took a deep breath. Yes, it was good to be back!

Peter Willey was there just across the room, his kit immaculately laid out as usual. He had shocked the club by relinquishing the captaincy during the winter following last year's highly publicised dressing room dramas, which largely revolved around him and Philip De Freitas. I was interested by the criticism of De Freitas on the New Zealand leg of England's tour. He was rebuked for exactly the kind of attitude which had frustrated Willey last season: lack of effort, and lack of interest in the team's well being, except when it suited him.

Willey eventually dropped him, which brought media sympathy for

Daffy, and caused a split in the team. There were those who thought that Daffy should be cossetted and helped, and others like me, who felt that he was letting us all down. Professional cricket is hard graft. Success only comes through practice and effort on the field and De Freitas must be made to realise that. It seemed a travesty to many of us when Daffy was selected to tour for England during the winter.

I had had my best ever season, taken 101 wickets, and yet was overlooked. I remember the stony silence in the dressing room when John Culley, our local newspaper reporter, poked his head around the door and told us that Daffy was in, and I was not. If my team mates were disappointed for me, imagine how I felt. I know that De Freitas was embarrassed when I congratulated him. He knew and I knew that I did not really mean it. I hope that he has learnt his lesson from last year. He is not back yet; the England team only arrived home this morning.

It will be interesting to see how Peter Willey fits into things this season. He is a close friend, and I was shattered when he quit as captain. I know that he was deeply hurt by all the wranglings off the field last year, although he would never admit it. But at times he did little to help himself. Things are either black or white to Will, there is nothing in between. I remember cringeing on several occasions when he dealt with someone tactlessly. Just a little thought or discretion would have made all the difference. I think he will have a great season. He is a highly respected pro and a magnificent player, and I think that without the burden of the captaincy he will play with more freedom. We will certainly be without David Gower for much of the season when he is involved with England, and it is vital for our chances of success that Willey scores runs.

The same could be said of James Whitaker, an England tourist two winters ago. He had problems with his approach to the game last year, and failed to fulfil his enormous potential. He became too involved with the off-the-field politics. He really does need to do the business this summer if he is to resurrent his international career.

But for now, the season still seems a long way off. The conversation is typical dressing room banter; gentle leg-pulling, with Peter Such's new hair style coming under particular scrutiny. It is an extraordinary sight, a cross between something out of Top Of the Pops and an exhibit on Gardener's World. Les is busy showing everyone his new bat, hot off the press at Duncan Fearnley's factory. "That'll be good for a hundred this year," he insists. He means for the season.

Good natured stuff . . . but usually it does not last long. For now there are no pressures, no selection problems, and people are just happy to be back at work after the long winter. David Gower's headaches will begin the moment he pins up the team to play Oxford University at The Parks on April 16.

Gower is even less fit than either myself or Les. He has had a complete break from cricket for the past six months, and it certainly showed today. After an early spurt along the canal towpath, it was not long before Les and I, bringing up the rear as usual, spotted him walking and breathing heavily. As we both hate to see the captain struggling, we agreed to walk the remaining mile and a half with him to keep him company. That bloody tow path has been extended.

We talked about our three-day trip to the Isle of Wight on Sunday, which will include discussions with a doctor about mental preparation and relaxation. Gower is a big believer in the power of the mind.

Training was as hard as I had feared. When we eventually arrived at the Polytechnic we had a strenuous stretching session followed by a circuit, which involves a lot of work with weights. We only do it for a few days and then never pick up the weights again, so the obvious side effect of weight training is that everyone gets very stiff for days afterwards which severely affects the quality of the nets sessions.

I would rather do plenty of running, with lots of sprint work. But as usual my protests fell on deaf ears, and we did the circuit. Everyone will be very stiff tomorrow which will mean the nets will be a waste of time. Later we ran/walked back along the canal, and had two and a half hours of indoor nets. I was reasonably happy with the way I bowled considering it was my first effort for six months. There were several new and incredibly young-looking faces. Funny to think that ten years ago I was in their position with all the uncertainty and excitement that went with it.

It was a hard day for everyone, but summed up by Peter Willey's caustic comment echoing from the showers as I left the dressing room: "That's another bloody day nearer to retirement!"

24 March

Daffy turned up today — a good effort, because there no need for him to do so. He looks well, and after the usual ribbing about his suntan he had a net. It coincided with my turn to bat, and immediately he ripped one into my already stiff right thigh. That amused Willey of course. It was good to see De Freitas so keen to join us; hopefully a sign of things to come.

His problems last season came to a head with the celebrated "salt throwing, kit lobbing" incident during our match with Sussex. This what happened.

I had been ill for several days, unable to eat anything, and the chef at the ground prepared a light fish dish specially for me. I was only out of bed in case I was needed to bat to save the match. Then along comes Daffy and empties the contents of a salt cellar all over it. I exploded. I threw all his kit over the balcony of our dressing room. I remember watching all the members diving for cover as boots, pads and, eventually, his bat crashed down among them.

Mainly I was angry because it was Daffy again showing such scant regard for anyone else. The problem quickly got worse because Daffy and Will had words which ended with Will threatening to deposit Daffy over the balcony with the rest of his kit. Daffy then stormed out of the ground and went home. And we were on a run chase at the time.

Panic set in as the Press became aware of the situation. Mike Turner's son was dispatched to Wigston to collect Daffy, but returned empty-handed. It was then a case of the mountain going to Mohammed, as Turner himself drove out of the ground, watched by an increasingly bemused crowd.

An hour or so later a ripple of excited chatter broke out among the spectators and there was Daffy at the top end of the ground jogging in through the car park gate. Reporters surrounded him as he neared the pavilion. But they failed to notice the sleek form of Turner's Jag slipping into the official's car park via another entrance.

"What's up? I've just been for a run," said Daffy innocently. In fact he went out to bat, after seriously warning me never to talk to him again, and won us the game by smashing 26 in no time.

The eventual reason for Daffy's omission from the team was simply on grounds of performance. He was not getting wickets, and George Ferris, in the second team, was. Thus the career of the most flamboyant cricketer to break through since Ian Botham was at a crossroads. Last season ended with him threatening to leave Leicestershire.

That he has enormous talent is beyond question and it would be criminal if it went to waste. He is a completely natural cricketer, who has the ability to turn the course of a match within a few minutes with either bat or ball. He is a crowd puller, too.

I hope he has learnt by his mistakes. Gower, I think, will treat him differently. He will cajole him and let him have his own way. That may work, but it may also annoy the other players in the team if he gets his own way all the time. There is no denying that 1988 is a vital year in the career of one P.A.J. De Freitas.

26 March

We had our first team meeting this afternoon to sort out the details of the Isle of Wight trip. Gower was at his eloquent best, stressing the importance of the three days. The mornings are to be spent training with Craig Mortimer, our physio, and the afternoons with the good doctor, dealing with the mental side of playing a professional sport.

I wonder how the likes of Will and Daffy are going to take to the idea. Gower, in deadly earnest, encouraged us to take our Walkmans along, as a motivation tape has been specially prepared for each of us.

I am transport organiser as usual, which means sorting out the car list and travel arrangements. It sounds simple, but always causes arguments. Some people don't want to travel with others, and non smokers don't want smokers in their cars, and so on. I eventually struck a successful formula consisting of seven cars taking three players each. But it will be a miracle if everybody gets to Lymington at 1.30 on Sunday in time to catch the ferry.

Les and I decided that we would run to the Poly. Regret set in when we found ourselves splashing through a foot of mud, but we made the four miles and felt much better for it. It is amazing what only two days of training can do. On the way down Les told me about his preparations for his benefit next year. He is the sort of bloke you hope will have a really good benefit, an honest county cricketer with only a couple of England caps, who has never made any more than a living from the game. It is rumoured that David Gower, who must earn five or six times more than Les, made something approaching £120,000 from his benefit last year. Someone like Les could expect maybe £40,000 if he is lucky. It does not seem fair.

Making ends meet is a constant worry for most cricketers, particularly those with a family and a mortgage. Only two Leicestershire players are paid more than £10,000 a year — and I am not one of them. The club's argument is that you are being paid for six months work, so you have another six months to double your pay. It's a great theory ... In reality players end up doing all kinds of dead end jobs to see them through the winter, assuming they can get a job at all. Les Taylor has worked in a quarry in the in the past, but last winter he was on the dole. So was Peter Willey. I spent one winter driving a lorry ... and almost killed myself when the steering failed on a steep bend. The only way to get the old thing up to 40 miles an hour was to stand up with all your weight on the accelerator. After a bit you got tired so you swapped feet. Another year I knocked windows together for a local manufacturing company. It was so boring.

I spent four winters playing and coaching in Australia and Zimbabwe. It's good fun ... but it doesn't pay. You just about get enough to cover your living costs out there but there is nothing left over to pay the mortgage back home. On my last trip to Australia I was paid around £1,500 for six months.

Financially, the only place to be is in the England squad. Test players earn nearly £2,000 a match and around £15,000 for a tour. It's a different league.

I think I will be bowling in a wheelchair by the time my benefit comes around! 1994 it is due. I am a member of the select band who was capped by England before my county. I know Geoff Miller is a member. I think Graham Dilley is too, but there are not many of us.

The training was conducted along exactly the same lines as yesterday, with lots of competitive sprints. We were allocated to the same teams too — Agnew, Taylor, Such and Potter. No price! It meant yet more punitive press ups! Les had a nightmare in goal during the five-a-side football

KEEPER'S BALL: *Les hangs on to one at last.* Leicester Mercury

contest to cap a desperate morning for the Agnew team. Twice he conceded freakish goals by clearing the ball straight on to an opponent, with the ball rebounding and trickling back into his own goal. Great "what happened nexts" for *A Question Of Sport*. My day finished by being bowled by James Whitaker in the nets. Say no more!

27 March

We are on the Isle of Wight in a large country house style of hotel, which was the retreat of the poet Tennyson. It seems a great place to come and get away from it all, which is hardly what we had in mind.

I put one newcomer in every car where possible for the journey down so he could get more comfortable with the senior players. I brought Martin Gidley. He's just got three 'A' levels and a place at university, but he seems dead keen to make a go of cricket. I hope it works out for him. Too many talented young players in his position opt for the security of university, and then a job away from the game, rather than gambling on a future in professional cricket.

Russell Cobb came too and told me about his plans to become a commercial pilot. That made me extremely jealous as I have always wanted to learn to fly. He spends his winters in South Africa, and seems to think that he could get his wings over there next year. Compared to the other cricketers I know who hold flying licences — Ian Botham and Colin Croft — Cobby would have my trust every time! He needs a good season this year. He is still on the fringe of the first team because he seems to be unable to adapt to one-day cricket. He is a solid opening bat, but never dominates a bowling attack. If it does not all happen for him this year I think he may quit.

We met the doctor, Martin Landau- North, this evening. Mike Turner described him as a psychologist. After talking to him, I feel sure that he could do something for my self confidence and positive thought. He said that he would be happy to see me privately during the season. The general feeling is that he will be of some use.

It will be a busy day tomorrow. The media is descending on us, and it will be interesting to see how much mileage they get out of Leicestershire's cricketers consulting a shrink!

28 March

Today I was hypnotised by Martin. It was an amazing experience. We began with a group session, and within minutes he had put half the team into a trance. Tim Boon was actually snoring. It did nothing for me at this stage, but I was fascinated by the reaction of the others. Martin talked at length about positive thought and had a go at curing my main batting problem; a lack of confidence against fast bowlers following a nasty blow in the mouth several years ago. He got me to look at the positive side of things. I had not been hit since, and had managed to score runs off fast bowlers. It will be interesting to see if it makes a difference.

What convinced me that he can be of benefit was his exhibition this evening. I suggested it might help some of the sceptics if he fully hypnotised some of us and proved what he could do. After dinner ten of us returned to the Tennyson library. First he put our physio Craig under, and showed us that although he was in deep hypnosis, he was fully aware of everything around him. Martin told Craig that when he woke up, he would think that his feet and shoes were wet through. Sure enough, he came to pulling faces, and wiggling his feet as if to dry them. Then it was my turn. Martin told me to close my eyes. Then he started counting, and I felt myself floating away, but still conscious. When he stopped counting, at about number eleven, I felt totally relaxed. But as soon as he resumed the count I felt a sort of gripping sensation around my face dragging me further under. Martin lifted my left arm, which was like lead. I could feel him doing it, but could do nothing to stop him. A couple of the lads came up and did the same. Before Martin brought me round he suggested to my subconscious that I say "Viv Richards can hit me on the head," a throwback to our discussion during the afternoon. Sure enough I found myself saying it as I came to,

21

much to the lads' amusement!

I feel the whole trip is turning out to be a great success. Our training this morning was fun but hard, starting with a run along the cliffs, and finishing at a magnificent sports centre for sprints and a bit of football. The highlight was Les falling down a rabbit hole on the run along the cliffs. Team spirit is better than I have ever known it, and I have the feeling that this is going to be Leicestershire's year. It is just up to the players to believe it. That is Martin's job.

29 March

I really am into hypnosis. I have been under four times today, once with Martin, who taped it at the same time, and the others after listening to the tape. Even Peter Willey seems intrigued by it, although he refuses to be hypnotised. The only person to speak out against it is De Freitas, which is to be expected. Everyone else appears to rate it, so he has to rebel against the general flow. Martin appreciates that, and tried to involve Daffy more in this afternoon's session. Daffy then felt that he was centrally involved again ... and responded.

Today's session included an hysterical outburst against something that I have done for ten years — sitting on the fence at fine leg between balls and talking to the crowd. I do this for a number of reasons; to have a bit of a breather while I am bowling, because chatting to a member of the crowd relaxes me and as a bit of a public relations exercise. Many people have come up to me after a match, particularly when we are playing away, and said how much they have enjoyed watching Leicestershire because we are such a friendly bunch. Those are the people who will come and watch us again.

Anway, it seems this irritates a lot of people, and I still cannot understand why. Who the hell is interested in how fine leg passes the time between balls? Why does it annoy the likes of De Freitas so much?

I think it is the easiest way he knows of having a gentle stab at me to make up for the jibes I make at him. He got really fired up this afternoon.

The others said that they thought it looked unprofessional. We seem to have reached an impasse. But I know that wherever our first match is later next month, I will be there in my customary position. I hope that the others are making more of an effort to ensure they are in the right frame of mind rather than worrying about me.

That took up most of the afternoon's meeting and I felt it was a waste of valuable time. Martin left this evening promising to teach me how to hypnotise myself when he came to Leicester later in the season. I can't wait for my positive thinking tape to arrive.

Today's real disappointment was losing ten quid to James Whitaker on the snooker table. We play regularly on away trips, and are pretty evenly matched, but I felt robbed today! An Agnew foul on the black clinched the match for Whitaker, who was his normal unbearably chirpy self when he won. When I went to the bar before dinner, most of the lads were in there, except for James. He had obviously been waiting and followed me in to be greeted by rapturous applause. It cost him an enormous round of drinks though!

Les got his just reward as well today. On our run this morning, he and I decided on a bit of a detour. It was a little bit shorter than the proper route. As we were heading away from the main bunch, crouching down and laughing like schoolboys, Les stepped in the biggest pile of dog crap I have ever seen. He is still trying to scrape it off his shoe this evening. They are quite right you know, cheating never pays.

30 March

What an awful day! Five and a half hours it took to get back to Leicester because of road works. It could have been even worse, because we almost missed the ferry too. Willey had made it on board, but there was a serious possibility that the Agnew contingent would have to wait an hour for the next crossing. Anyway, Will positioned himself on the top deck right above the car boarding area, and in full view of us on the quay, desperately hoping that we would miss the boat, so to speak, and he could wave goodbye to us all the way to Lymington. His plan failed. We were the last car allowed on.

I hypnotised myself this evening in front of Bev, who said that I looked stupid! She was probably right. The sessions with Martin were taken far more seriously than I thought they would be, and I believe that several players will have benefited from the trip. It was also good for team morale after the divisions of last season. I am pleased for Mike Turner, who battled with the committee to get the trip organised. It will be intriguing to see if Martin's ideas have any effect on our performances during the coming season.

31 March

Some people were not satisfied with the entertainment provided for us at the Farringford Hotel, and made their own arrangements. A fire extinguisher was let off in one of the rooms. It was hardly a major crime, as Gower said during our meeting to find the culprit, but Mike Turner was owed £27 for a replacement. It was a couple of the new lads, which I am sure Gower knew anyway. This was a clever ploy to make them feel embarrassed in front of the senior players. Anyway it was left that £27, or greenbacks as Gower kept calling them, would be on the table in the dressing room at 9.30 on Tuesday morning.

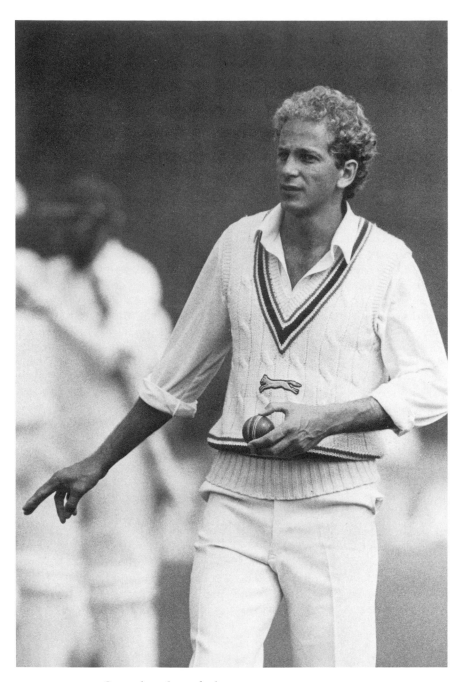

I'M IN CHARGE: Gower lays down the law.

David Munden

It was a hard day, with hours of indoor nets. My first ball hit the side netting, which is never a very good sign. The problem with indoor nets is that the bowlers only have about a four pace run up, and the surface is so good that after a few minutes even the most inept batsman can strike the ball on the up, and look like Don Bradman (except Peter Such, who still looks like Peter Such!). This really frustrates the bowlers, and provokes the concrete delivery. This is a bouncer, but it really skids off the indoor surface. I have never seen so many concrete deliveries bowled as there have been this year, with Justin Benson, a youngster known as Rambo, being the main culprit. He is crafty though — he only bounces batsmen who cannot give it back when it is his turn to bat.

5 April

I spent the weekend moving house, which means that everything I need is stuck in a tea chest somewhere. I have lost my very expensive indoor cricket shoes, but something I did find today was the bottom half of my favourite tracksuit which disappeared three years ago. It turned up this afternoon in the nets on Les Taylor.

I could not believe it. Somehow he had come by these trousers three years ago, and had not dare wear them until today. The nets session came to a grinding halt as we had a minor slanging match. He denied that they were mine, until I asked him to produce the top half, which I knew was in my bag in the dressing room. We had a good laugh about it all afterwards, and decided that the trousers were a better fit on him anway. Les and I have been mates for too long for a spot of petty larceny to break up our relationship.

I had driven into Grace Road with my heater still on the highest setting, and could not believe my eyes. The lads were in the outside nets even though it was freezing and blowing a gale. It is vital to grab every bit of outside practice you can at this stage because it might be the only chance you get before the first match. I was very conscious of that as I got changed, knowing that in only ten days time I would be running in to bowl at Chris Broad and Tim Robinson at Lord's for the MCC against Notts. And they have both been away on tour all winter. That match is vitally important for me, if I am not to be written off as a one-season wonder. I asked David Gower how much importance the selectors placed on that match. He said that they realise that you are probably very short of outdoor practice. That match is weighing heavily on my mind. I have rarely bowled well at Lord's.

6 April

I do not think I have ever been colder when trying to play cricket than I was today. A raw northerly swept across Grace Road, as we attempted to have a sensible net. The top has gone off the wicket now, which means that the ball tends to rear off a length. If that happened in August, the batsmen would all be moaning, and refusing to have a net. But now they are dead keen to get on with things and the odd throat ball is laughed off.

I have been studying David Gower closely these past two weeks. He spent the winter well away from cricket, hoping to recharge his batteries and he certainly seems very keen. Today while he was batting something quite unusual happened. Higgy shouted "last round", meaning the last four or five balls for the batsmen before changing round, and Gower played the first of these into the net, about half way up the pitch. He walked up and picked up the ball. Last year he would certainly have walked out of the net, not bothering to face the remaining three or four deliveries, but this time, he went back and took strike. I was most impressed, and said so when he eventually came out. The answer was quite simple: he had not heard Higgy shout "last round!" Tonight's forecast is for more freezing weather with strong winds. I can feel a strained hamstring coming on.

7 April

I was involved in an extremely embarrassing incident today, although the more I think about it, the more I feel I was set up. I was chatting to Les as we walked back to our bowling markers, when I produced a handkerchief. Les immediately asked me where I had got it and claimed it had his initial in the corner. He snatched it, and sure enough, there was a very nicely embroidered itallic 'L'. Les triumphantly stuck it into the pocket of his tracksuit bottom, which of course was really mine. I have been done. Outsmarted. Action will be taken.

Once again the forecasters got it wrong. Today was an absolute beauty. Nets were almost enjoyable. I got down to only three sweaters, which meant that I was able to bowl with more freedom. My strength is my ability to swing the ball, and conditions have not been suitable for that yet, but I am bowling in roughly the right spot five times an over.

My batting is awful, though. If anyone had watched me today, they would have thought that I had never held a bat before. Ken Higgs clean bowled me twice, and James Whitaker beat me several times outside the off stump. Things are not good.

Agnew got on the scoresheet twice in the nine-a-side football match after training. We won 4–2, thanks to very little skill, and some fortunate goal hanging by the author. Les was brilliant in goal, until he let one trickle through his legs. It is good to win the football, because there are a couple of the lads who are very reasonable players indeed, notably Phil Whitticase and Lloyd Tennant. They always play in the same team, and take it very seriously. They lost today, and were far from impressed. Of course Les and I did not rub it in very much.

26

There is the first sign of a major split in the team ... over a television in the dressing room. It is a "thank you" present to the players from David Gower for our help in his benefit last year, and it is already causing a lot of ill-feeling. It is as if the TV is an excuse for failure before the season starts. "There'll soon be a bat through that" is one of the more common remarks at the moment, and James Whitaker seems paranoid about the thing. Cricket does involve a lot of sitting about, especially for lower order batsmen, and people relax in different ways. From my experience of Test matches, the TV is always on, and very rarely on the actual match itself. It helps to break the tension. Those who want to concentrate can go outside, and the others can relax. As usual it is a question of give and take. There is not a lot of that in professional cricket.

11 April

I am one of the five *Wisden* Cricketers of the Year, it was announced today. After playing for England, it is the biggest honour available in the game. I remember looking through my *Wisdens* when I was a kid and seeing photos of all my heroes as Cricketers of The Year. The official dinner is tomorrow evening in London, and I hope that a couple of the England selectors will also be there. The other winners are Neil Foster, Peter Roebuck, David Hughes and Salim Malik. Fossie and I are good friends, and I have not seen him for ages. I want to give him some stick for his hair do on *A Question of Sport* the other day. He looked like a toilet brush. We always have a contest to see who is the thinnest. It is very close I can tell you.

We had a couple of good sessions with Martin about pressure. In a tight situation, we must make the opposition feel under pressure rather than ourselves. He has suggested a key word that Gower must shout on the field when things are tight, and that is "shovel". It is supposed to automatically make us think that we are shovelling a heap of horse manure, representing the pressure, on to the batsmen. I can see the reasoning, I am just not too sure of the word. I can imagine Dickie Bird's face if our skipper suddenly bellowed "shovel" loud enough for Les to hear. I think the batsmen might be a little confused too! Some are also keen on putting up a sign in the pavilion like Liverpool have in the tunnel at Anfield. The sign there simply says This is Anfield, which reminds the opposition that they are about to enter the lion's den, and puts them at a psychological disadvantage. I am not in favour of having the same sort of thing in our pavilion, but Daffy in particular thinks it will work. Daffy was one of the major contributors today. We learnt that sometimes he feels that he has to explode to get something off his chest, and then it is all forgotten, and also that he likes encouragement on the field most of the time, but sometimes hates it. Tricky one that. I am not sure who is going to have to test the water and risk getting a mouthful! He is a very complicated character, but I think we are all getting to know him better.

After the session Martin hypnotised me, and did a special tape for me. I have always had problems with self confidence, and I can feel myself getting uptight about the MCC match already. I will listen to the tape every day until the match, and see if it does me any good. He also showed me how to hypnotise myself.

One interesting observation. I went to the dressing room after lunch. There was only one other person in there, and he was watching the new TV. James Whitaker.

12 April

The night of the *Wisden* awards at the East India Club in St James' Square. It was the right place for the occasion, full of tradition, with oak panelled lounges for Gentlemen Only. I met Peter Lush on the way in. A really nice fellow. He was the manager of the ill-fated England B Tour in 1986 of which I was a member. It was dogged by political problems. I was impressed at the time by his calmness in a crisis, and also his reluctance to get involved with cricket matters. He was not a professional player, and so leaves that to his assistant. Since then, of course, he has become England's Tour Manager.

Everybody who is anybody in cricket journalism was there. I have always enjoyed their company. I often spend an hour or two in the press box during a match. Jim Swanton, Brian Johnston and Trevor Bailey all offered me genuine congratulations on my award. Star-gazer Patrick Moore headed the list of personalities. I have always enjoyed him on TV. As I introduced myself nervously to him I was unaware how keen he was on cricket. "You don't need introducing to me, I've seen you play several times," he said. "Make sure you show those idiot selectors what a mistake they made, and force your way back into the England side. Good luck." I was quite taken aback, and flattered.

At dinner I was placed next to Sir Gubby Allen. 86 years old, but as bright as could be, and fascinating company. We discussed the Bodyline Tour. He told Douglas Jardine that he was totally opposed to leg theory. It must have been a very difficult decision, because he was Jardine's best friend. We talked about Harold Larwood and Don Bradman, and how they would compare to contemporary cricketers. He was the first player from "the old days" to whom I could talk seriously about modern cricket without the customary: "It was so much better in my day" that we seem to hear all the time. The likes of Fred Trueman seem to seriously believe that nobody these days has the first idea how to bowl. I feel very strongly about Trueman, who could have been so helpful to my generation of fast bowlers. Instead he never misses the chance to criticise us, and tell everyone what a great cricketer he was. He might well have been, but it really is a shame that he has such an enormous chip on his shoulder. What makes me laugh is the way he comes out every year offering help, and giving the impression that he is incredibly hurt. The truth is that no one will go near him, and it is totally his doing. It is such a waste. Gubby was completely different, and because of that, I talked to him about swing bowling. It turns out that our styles are very similar, although his record is rather better than mine! We compared field settings and gripping the ball. Two players whose careers are half a century apart finding that perhaps the game has not really changed that much after all. He told me what Len Hutton had said to him when he first started.

"Allen, you are very fortunate young man. You move the ball both ways. I don't like the ball to move both ways outside my off stump, and if I don't like it, the rest of the team certainly won't!" That was the moment when Gubby realised that there was more to bowling than hurling the ball down as fast as possible, and started to concentrate on swinging it. Exactly what I had discovered last year. As I drove up the M1 in the small hours I glanced at my complimentary copy of *Wisden* on the passenger's seat. I had got Gubby to sign it as a momento.

13 April

Nets are becoming a pain in the rear. We have been outside for a week now but it seems like a year and it is affecting everyone. People are edgy and aggressive. I think that it is because of our early reporting date this year. There has been too long a wait for the first game. We all want action now. Batsmen get bored after ten of fifteen minutes in the net, and start to play outrageous shots. The bowlers then start to lark around and the whole thing breaks down. After slogging away for an hour and a half this afternoon I turned round to see Peter Such and Guy Lovell, an even worse batsman than Such, getting their pads on for their second innings of the day. That was it. I set off for the pavilion. Bowling at Suchy twice in a day is too much for anyone, except of course in a match, when I would be delighted to see him at the crease.

At least I am now happy with the way I am bowling. I have got my slower ball back.

14 April

Real cricket at last! We had a practice match out in the middle. Each batsman batted for half an hour and the bowlers bowled for about an hour at a time. It was extremely competitive and several tempers were frayed. De Freitas was slogged all over the park, and thoroughly lost his rag. Peter Willey destroyed Les Taylor, and they both had words. Cobby and I had a hard tussle too. But it got rid of the aggression and we were all friends again afterwards.

It is so different in the middle, especially for the bowlers. There is suddenly an umpire standing there, and there is the feeling of enormous space around you. I bowled well and got a couple of wickets, with the odd rusty half volley thrown in. But the best on the day was Chris Lewis, an English West Indian, who toured Australia with Young England during the winter. He uses a short run, but can bowl a very quick ball, and he swings it too. I think he will go a long way. There is great competition between him and Daffy, and Lewis certainly won today's battle.

The team for Oxford was posted with no surprises. Of course I am not included which relieves the pressure on the selection of the bowlers. Daffy, Les and Lewis are the seamers with Peter Such and Willey for spin. When we get to Derby next Thursday for our first four-day match, Suchy might miss out, and we will play four fast bowlers. I feel confident about the MCC game at the weekend, but cautiously so. I feel that eveyone is willing me to do well and I am determined I will not let them down.

15 April

The eve of a new season. What will it bring? Another 100 wickets? An England recall? Will it be my last year of professional cricket? Basically the same thoughts every cricketer will be having this evening, except probably the last one.

I am really looking forward to tomorrow, I checked in to the Westmoreland Hotel, besides Lord's, and met some of my team mates in the bar. All old friends. Leicestershire's trip to The Isle of Wight was talked about, particularly the part concerning Martin. Word seems to have spread.

My feelings about the coming season are straightforward this evening. Playing cricket is what I do best, and I feel I have enormous public support. Right now I cannot see myself as anything else other than a professional cricketer, yet a couple of months ago I felt like a journalist. It is all so complicated. I want to listen to Martin's cassette tonight. The next three days could set the course for the whole season. It is a frightening thought.

CHAPTER TWO

April Showers

16 April

Nottinghamshire 125 for 1: Robinson 62 not out; Broad 49
v MCC

No wickets, but several moral victories. I am pleased with the way I bowled. Robinson and Broad were obviously in reasonable nick, but both Small and I beat the bat on many occasions and had Robbo dropped as well.

The start was delayed because of miserable light rain, but that gave us a settling-in period. Good for the nerves. Nick Cook and Graeme Fowler were both in excellent form in the dressing room, and it was not long before everyone felt part of the set up.

I was asked to do an interview for TV AM while we were waiting. It seemed straightforward enough, talking about the new season, until suddenly:

"Don't you feel you are holding the Selectors to ransom by threatening to quit unless they pick you for England?"

I felt my knees tremble a little, and I can't remember what I said to get out of that one.

The selectors were all in the pavilion. Peter May gritted his teeth, and said well done for last season. Micky Stewart was there too, and we chatted about my radio work. Fred Titmus totally ignored me as usual. He and I go back a long way; to 1977 and The Oval to be exact. I was on a schoolboy arrangement, playing in the summer holidays, and Titmus was the county coach. I do not think he rated me as a bowler — something he told the Middlesex players a few years later when he made a comeback for them against us. I remember once having a problem with no balls, and I asked his advice. "Get in the bloody nets, and sort it out," was his reply.

GRAEME FOWLER: A duck ... and loads of sauce.   Graham Morris

Leicestershire offered me a proper contract for 1978, and I grabbed it. Surrey did not even seem to notice. They did not write me, or make any contact, until I had made my debut for Leicestershire. I did well and found myself on the way to Australia on a Whitbread Scholarship. Then they accused Leicestershire of poaching me, which of course was not true. About the same time Titmus resigned. Perhaps letting me slip through his fingers was part of the reason. From that day to this Titmus has ignored me totally.

I dined with Jack Russell in the hotel this evening. He is a very conscientious professional and an extremely talented wicketkeeper. But he lacks confidence, as an incident today showed. Robinson edged Small low to first slip, where Mark Nicholas shelled it. Russell reckoned that if he had been playing for Gloucestershire he would have gone for the ball and probably caught it, even though strictly it was not his. He is on the verge of Test cricket, and clearly wants to do well this season. I gave him Martin's phone number.

It does not matter how many nets you have or how many miles you run during pre-season training, the first few matches are hard work. I feel shattered this evening, but certainly in better shape than the new digital scoreboard which was unveiled today. A whole line of arabic graphics appeared across the top, and would not go away. Apparently the machinery had got wet. Lord's first step into the twentieth century ... I cannot help but feel that it was never meant to work!

17 April

Nottinghamshire 298 for 3 declared: Robinson 129; Johnson 61 not out; Agnew 1 for 71
MCC 159 for 7: Hick 61

Disappointing. I eventually got a wicket — Robinson caught behind — but then their seamers ripped our batting apart. Apart from Graeme Hick we played abysmally and very nearly followed on. Again, I was reasonably happy with my bowling, but I hoped that their bowlers would be made to struggle too. Franklyn Stephenson bowled bloody fast this evening. He is a very tall gangling man, and while I cannot see him filling Richard Hadlee's shoes, he certainly bowls at a mean speed. Like all the West Indian "fast and nasties" who seem intent on death and destruction on the field of play, Frankie is a lovely, almost comical character off it. He has a near impossible task at Notts this season.

My mate Graeme Fowler started 1988 with a duck. He laughed it off as always. He forgot his thigh pad, which is still in Jamaica apparently, where Lancashire had their pre-season tour, so he borrowed Chris Broad's. With only ten minutes between innings, the opening batsmen are always rushed to get all their kit on while the rest of us relax. The silence was suddenly shattered by Fowler's high-pitched Lancashire voice: "I can't wear that bloody thing. It's like having a policeman's riot shield stuffed down your trousers!" So he went without.

The new scoreboard was still displaying the unusual arabic message across it. We reckoned it was Kuwaiti for "Welcome to Lord's!" An antiquated thing on wheels had been pushed round to fine leg to act as substitute.

Had a very enjoyable Italian meal this evening with several players plus Leicestershire's fanatical supporter Robin Asquith, the actor of Confessions fame. A very funny bloke, and excellent company.

Chris Broad was there, too, and gave his explanation of his "stumps flattening" episode in the Bi-Centennial test in Sydney. After a couple of glasses of wine, he found himself under interrogation, and said that the whole incident was accidental. He had raised his bat to allow the ball to pass, but the ball hit his arm and went on to the wicket. Then gravity took over. The bat just dropped, and happened to hit the wicket. I am not entirely convinced, and nor were the others.

After several more glasses of wine I retired to bed, not exactly relishing the thought of fending off Franklyn in the morning. After a few drinks you imagine yourself playing every shot in the book. Ah well, dreams are cheap.

18 April

Nottinghamshire 298 for 3 dec and 139 for 2 dec: Johnson 59 not out;
Agnew 2 for 43
MCC 159 for 7 dec and 222 for 5. Fowler 73
Match drawn

Our batsmen got it together today, with Graeme Fowler playing really well. We were still 57 short, but at least the game was entertaining.

We declared overnight, so Cooky and I were spared our first encounter with Franklyn Stevenson.

I did not bowl well, which was frustrating because it was humid with a breeze in the perfect direction for me to swing it. I could not get the ball in the right place often enough. I got Robinson and Broad. Robbo was caught at square cover off the back of the bat from a ball which bounced a bit more, and Broad was even more unlucky. He edged one down the leg side and was caught by Russell. Luck is on my side at the moment. I felt very tired because Colin Wells was unable to bowl with a strained back which meant nearly 40 overs in the match for me. I bowled a few loose deliveries today which were smashed for four, mainly by Paul Johnson, who showed again what a fine player he is. I remember mentioning his name in a TV interview during a rain-hit Sunday League match as a player for the future. Johnson can be a bit loose, but he has got every shot in the book, and times it beautifully. Mind you, Graeme Hick is something else. It is easy to say what a great player someone is when you see him score a double hundred. I missed Hick's 61 in the first innings, but I saw him score 37 today. What a 37! Somehow, we have always got rid of him cheaply at Leicester and so I had not really seen him going. I have never witnessed talent like it, and that includes the likes of Gower. Hick stands up so straight. If the ball is slightly wide it is smashed square on the off side, and anything pitched up goes like a rocket straight. Oh yes, he also hooked two sixes into the stand off Saxelby! He has that streak of arrogance every top player needs, and will obviously score millions. He has already got over twenty first class hundreds, and he is only 22.

Game over. I didn't disgrace myself, but I didn't set the world alight either. I was rusty, and bowling against two players who were in good nick. If I had not got wickets later in the season in similar conditions, I would feel very upset, but I do not think that I have done my chances of playing for England any harm and I would have settled for that on Friday evening.

Meanwhile at The Parks, the lads have done the usual job on Oxford University. They were bowled out for a 98 with Lewis and De Freitas both taking four wickets, and in reply we are 177 for three. Willey was caught for eight. He had been determined to score a century, but there is always one batsman who fails to cash in against the students. Will will not be happy, but I can think of a few who will be chuckling.

Cricket is so important to Will. The game is all he knows and he has no idea what he's going to do when he has to pack in. I think he will carry on playing until he drops. He jokes that when he is too old for Leicestershire, he will still have a couple of years left at Glamorgan, like everybody else.

20 April

I saw Daffy's new car today. *Very* smart. He had been trying to pass his test for ages but kept failing ... and a fleet of sponsored cars for the team depended on his ability to drive. Carphone, who sponsor Ian Botham, Worcestershire and Queensland, offered him not only a phone, but a car to put it in too! And in desperation Daffy booked a ticket to his native Dominica a couple of weeks ago, and passed a local test there. One does not like to question the standard of driving in Dominica, except it seems that the most common mode of transport is still the mule and cart. Believe it or not, Philip De Freitas is now the proud owner of a fully-sponsored, series three, petrol injected BMW. Heaven help whoever travels with him this season. It is a lovely machine, and he is very proud of it. I just hope they both look as sleek in September.

It was a day when both my jobs' paths crossed. After nets, I interviewed

David Gower for a promotion involving an incentive scheme for club cricketers. Basically, any club cricketer who scores a century this summer is entitled to a certificate signed by David, and there are special awards too, including one for the most unusual hundred scored. We reckoned Peter Such should be the judge for that.

I did the interview in a studio at Radio Leicester, the first time I have been back since the middle of March. A part of me does belong there.

Nets were a waste of time — green and bouncy. The batsmen were fighting for their lives, and it was not long before we abandoned the practice. Everyone seems confident that tomorrow is the first step on the long ladder towards the County Championship. I see we are currently quoted at 10 to 1 for the title. I think at those odds we are worth a few bob.

21 April

Britannic Assurance County Championship
Derbyshire 289 for 9: Maher 101 not out; Agnew 2 for 57

Derby! The very word sends a cold shudder down a cricketer's spine. The ground where there have been more reported cases of frostbite than any other first class venue. The ground so exposed that raw northerlies sweep straight in from the Arctic. The ground where the average County Championship match attracts no more than a couple of old dodderers, who seem barely alive. The ground where the visiting team's shower area is covered in slimy mould, with tiles hanging off the walls.

"It's like watching a fart go off," mused Les as he gazed out of the dressing room window. No one really understood what he meant exactly, but the place does inspire those sort of sentiments. Trust our luck to be here in mid April. Mind you it does mean that is nearly it for the season.

The pitch is damp and very slow, so Michael Holding was given the match off, and John Wright, the New Zealander, got a rare game. I had him early caught behind, and Leicestershire were soon in command. At one stage Derby were 87 for five, but they got off the hook, led by keeper Bernie Maher, and they must be delighted with their recovery. It was a very slow day's play, indicative of the pitch and conditions, but hardly a sparkling introduction to four-day cricket.

They blocked out the last half hour, waiting for the morning, yet if it had been a three-day game they would probably have declared and had a go at us. Their last man Devon Malcolm is a founder member of the Taylor and Such Batting Academy — so much so that Michael Holding has bet him that he will not score twenty in any single innings this season. If he does, Holding has to buy him dinner for a week. Devon is currently seven not out, and I have offered to enter a partnership arrangement with him. Holding has rumbled our plot.

TAKE THAT: Chris Lewis, pick of the bowlers.

David Munden

Chris Lewis was the pick of our bowlers today, taking four wickets to add to the ten he took in the Oxford match. I am a little concerned though that Gower is going to overbowl him. He was on for two hours either side of lunch — too much for a twenty year-old at this stage of the season. Daffy bowled well without taking a wicket, and by the end was getting desperate. He fails to understand that he can bowl magnificently one day and get nothing, and then pick up five wickets another day after bowling rubbish.

England selector Phil Sharpe was there too, which might have been on his mind. I do not know why. Sharpe watched me take eleven wickets there last season, but it did not seem to do me much good. I bowled 27 overs today, and feel extremely tired and sore. I might have felt a bit looser if I had been able to have a soak in the bath after the day's play. The showering facilities in the visitors side of the pavilion are a disgrace. There is damp everywhere, with mould all over the walls, and broken tiles litter the filthy floor. Clearly nothing had been touched since last year, and I lodged a protest with the Club Secretary. He played the innocent until I asked him if he would like to take a shower or bath in there. Then I was assured that they would be cleaned out first thing tomorrow.

22 April

Derbyshire 324 all out: Maher 121 not out; Lewis 5 for 73
Leicestershire 231 for 4: Briers 90; Whitaker 52 not out

Shortly after our arrival this morning, a little old man knocked on our dressing room door armed with a bucket and an assortment of bottles and aerosols and set about cleaning out our showers. He was in there for over two hours. At last we feel confident of taking a shower or bath without fear of contracting a serious disease.

Professional cricketers have a very simple means of gauging the temperature on the field of play. It is a "one sweater day" if there is brilliant sunshine, or a "two sweater day" if there is a bit of a chill in the breeze. Today was at least a seven sweater day. There was a biting wind and low cloud, with a top temperature of 48 degrees. Believe me, at Derby there is no escape. Dickie Bird resorted to raiding our dressing room when we were batting for spare long sleeved sweaters, and the cold had it's effect on John Hampshire as well. He forgot to replace the bails on the stumps after lunch, and no one noticed until Roger Finney was in full flight. Dickie dived into his path to prevent him from delivering the ball ... and the glare he gave Hamps will be remembered for a long time. I bet he never, ever, forgets to replace the bails again.

Devon Malcolm won his bet today. He scored 22, and so Holding must treat him to dinner for a week. Holding is claiming he never specified what the food had to be, and presented Devon with a loaf of bread. As I did not bowl today I am not eligible for a share.

Play ended early through bad light. If our batsmen had declined the offer to go off, they would have been lynched by both umpires, the Derbyshire team and the handful of spectators too. A colder day on the cricket field I cannot remember. The forecast for tomorrow is for a high of eight degrees. That is one degree colder than today. When will the powers that be consider a later start and finish to the season? This is no fun for anybody.

23 April

Derbyshire 324 all out and 66 for 0
Leicestershire 482 for 8 dec.: Whitaker 145; Potter 107

Today I bade farewell to one of my closest friends. Bertha, my faithful three pound willow, disintegrated while attempting something ferocious against Devon Malcolm. She had been with me through thick and thin for almost four years and her reputation went before her. Last year she nearly went into the record books with the fastest century of the season, and the best fast bowlers in the world have felt her wrath. Now, alas, she is no more, and after a short but moving ceremony conducted in the dressing room by Peter Willey, she was lobbed into the bin. My replacement, Chris Lewis's, proved equally as effective as I smashed Paul Newman for six and hit a couple of fours in a knock of 21 not out. Unfortunately Gower saw fit to deprive me of a certain hundred by declaring.

Dickie Bird is not a happy man. With an icicle hanging from the end of his nose, he perched in his uninimitable style, and said: "You wouldn't credit it Jonathan, (he and my parents are the only people in the world who always call me Jonathan), it's ruddy colder than yesterday. It's hell out here. Oslear found something in the rules to get off the pitch because of cold last year, but I can't find the bloody thing."

We didn't do too badly, though. James Whitaker played well for his 145, and Laurie Potter scored his first first class century for Leicestershire. He has never really established himself in our team since moving from Kent a couple of years ago, but he has always struck me as being a good player, and his confidence will be lifted now. I am sure he will score a heap of runs for us this year. Daffy's bad luck continues. Firstly he ran out Chris Lewis by most of the pitch, and only managed seven himself. Then he bowled really well into a strong wind this evening, but did not have the luck to get a wicket. His patience is being sorely tested. If this had happened at the same time last year, we would have had a tantrum by now. He seems to have learnt something.

I have an awful feeling that we will be in the field all day on Monday and the match will be a tedious draw. But that is two days away. Our Sunday campaign starts tomorrow, and last year we had an appalling run. I have a feeling that either Les or I could miss out in favour of a batter who bowls a bit and I will not be terribly upset if it is me. Sundays are a complete lottery, despised by the vast majority of players. Compare it to a day in the garden with the family and there is only one winner.

24 April

Refuge Assurance League

Leicestershire 168: Agnew 3
Derbyshire 171 for 1: Barnett 77 not out; Agnew 0 for 26
Derbyshire won by nine wickets

I got injured today, and it is worrying. The first weekend of the season and I'm on the physio's bench already. I threw in from fine leg, as I do probably twenty times a day, and it felt as if a red hot poker had been plunged into my right shoulder. In ten years of professional cricket I have never had any problem with my shoulders before, but it is very stiff indeed. The only treatment I can have at the moment is ice, because ultra sound cannot be used so soon after an injury. I-hope I am fit for Tuesday's crucial Benson and Hedges game against Lancashire.

The match itself was appalling. We did not even manage to bat for the full 40 overs. We lost Potter, Gower and Whitaker for less than twenty, and never recovered. Daffy batted well, but 169 was never going to be enough. We also fell foul of a ridiculous new rule: if a player leaves the field, a substitute fielder is not allowed for five overs. It was brought in because of the behaviour of the Pakistanis last summer. Today James Whitaker ricked his back badly while fielding and had to go off. It was obvious to everyone including the umpires that he was in agony, but we were not allowed a fielder to replace him. The match was at a critical stage and we could only have ten men on the field. It is a stupid rule, and it needs changing now. David Gower is writing to Lord's tonight in an attempt to get something done.

After the match Gower emphasised that we must change our approach to Sunday cricket. The batsmen tried to smack it about from the first ball. But the most important thing about batting in one day cricket is to have wickets in hand for the final charge. On Sundays, that is the last ten overs. Today we were vainly trying to hang in there and bat out the final overs, but we failed to do even that when Les had an almighty swipe and was cleaned up.

25 April

Derbyshire 324 and 331 for 8: Wright 84; Finney 52 not out; De Freitas 3 for 93; Willey 3 for 62
Leicestershire 482 for 8 dec

Match Drawn

We so nearly got that first win. It was good for morale ... that and the knowledge that we only have one more day at Derby this year! Daffy bowled superbly, and got his rewards this time. His first wicket was just what you would expect after much beating of the bat. Peter Bowler dragged on a wide one he was trying to leave alone. Daffy's face lit up and he was a different man. He bowled for an hour and a half as I was unfit.

I caught him out taking a breather during the afternoon, sitting on the fence at fine leg! I made sure that I chose my time to tell him what I had seen. I waited until he had taken a wicket, and announced it to the team. He blushed, then he laughed.

The wicket also took some spin, and Peter Willey bowled as well as I have ever seen him. With about 24 overs remaining, they had two wickets left, and a lead of only 120. We just could not get that vital wicket to get Devon Malcolm to the crease. Roger Finney and Paul Newman blocked it out until the close.

I got to the ground feeling depressed, my shoulder stiff and sore. I told Gower that my best chance of being fit for tomorrow was to take it easy today and have plenty of treatment from the physio. But because of that stupid new rule, I had to go on to the pitch for five overs as James could not field again. Gower then decided that I might as well stay on all day, in case I had to bowl in an emergency. I bowled the ball in from the boundary a couple of times, and it did not hurt. I will have to bowl flat out in the nets before the match starts to make sure that I am fully fit. It is the greatest sin a bowler can commit if he goes into a limited overs match less than 100 per cent fit, and not willing to go through the pain barrier to finish his overs. I am willing to do that if I know I am not doing any more damage to my shoulder. But there is too much of this season left to take silly risks.

26 April

Benson and Hedges Cup
Leicestershire 213 for 8: Willey 59; Boon 53; Agnew 5 not out
Lancashire 46 for 6 (19 overs)

Today we showed what a great side we can be, and why we should be in contention for all the major honours this season. Lancashire are on the rack, thanks to a magnificent team performance and a great effort by Daffy. He tore Lancashire's batting to shreds in a matter of four overs.

The wicket is green and very uneven but Lancashire's bowlers, with the exception of Paul Allott, did not look the part at all. Chris Matthews, the Australian, bowled a succession of wides and we were on the way to a massive score at 100 for one. Peter Willey then threw his wicket away on the stroke of lunch, and Trevor Jesty took five cheap wickets with his little floaters. A steady succession of batsmen trooped in and out, mainly succumbing to wide long hops, and being caught at the wicket. I went out to join Justin Benson, playing his first game for us in the place of the injured Whitaker, and there were still over three overs left. We ran singles until the last over came, and then Rambo cut loose taking 13 off it. He finished with an unbeaten 30 odd.

The difference that over made was crucial. The pressure switched straight away on to the Lancashire players and we all felt lifted. The ball seamed and swung, and there is definitely a ridge in the wicket bowling down the hill. Some balls Daffy bowled flew off a length, while others shot along the ground. If all our wickets play like that, we will win the Championship. I beat the bat countlessly and had Jesty, who is still there, dropped at slip. The whole team was on a high and I just hope that we can keep it going. I know it is hard to do because we are on the pitch for several hours at a time. It is easy to get charged up for a football match which only lasts for 90 minutes. Cricket is different, but when things go your way like today the bandwagon rolls. It was a great shame when the rain came after 19 overs. That was it for the day, despite some frantic efforts by umpire Don Oslear, who clearly wanted to get home this evening. The playing area was never going to be fit, but he kept us there until 7.15 in the hope that it would dry out. We return tomorrow to finish them off.

27 April

Leicestershire 213 for 8
Lancashire 167 all out: Jesty 57; De Freitas 4 for 27; Agnew 0 for 42

Leicestershire won by 46 runs

Everything so nearly went wrong. The last pair, Jack Simmons and Chris Matthews, put on 69 in 11 overs. They came out to play a few shots, and it paid off. There was an awful lot of tension on the field come the end, with Gower's captaincy being sorely tested for the first time this season. He coped well. When he was in charge the last time, he often blew a fuse on the field in a tight situation. Today he remained in control. My bowling took some hammer from the flailing bats. My attitude was wrong because, like everyone else, I thought we were home and dry when Matthews strode out at number eleven. I cannot afford any more lapses like that. Nigel

Briers had a few pointed things to say afterwards in the dressing room. He had not seen anyone having fielding practice before we went out, and the bowlers had not loosened up properly. Chris Lewis was not even on the ground when the umpires made the decision to start. Gower gave him a rocket when he sheepishly rushed into the dressing room with only minutes to go before the first ball. We have all learned a lesson I think. And we are ready for our arch-rivals Northampton tomorrow. I am preparing myself for my first Nedding of the year ...

28 April

Britannic Assurance County Championship
Northamptonshire 176 all out: Lamb 54; Agnew 6 for 66
Leicestershire 70 for 1

A mixture of great feelings; delight, relief, excitement. Six wickets were exactly what I needed with the selection for the One-Day Series against the West Indies only a couple of weeks away. Micky Stewart was there to see it. The pressure must be on the Selectors now. I have bowled better and had less to show for it, but after all the playing and missing at Derby. I deserved a change of luck. The ball swung, the wicket was green, but the only "strangle" was Allan Lamb, who played a short ball on to his stumps. Michael Carey, who writes for *The Independent*, said he felt I deserved the wickets, as he had been at Derby too.

So the Nedding did not take place. Let me explain. Ned is Wayne Larkins, the Northants opening bat. He plays every shot in the book from the word go, particularly when I am bowling. Last year at Grace Road he smashed my first ball, the first of the match, for four, and the second for six over cover! The ball disappeared down Milligan Road, and was never seen again. An assault by Larkins is now known in the Leicestershire dressing room as a Nedding. It has got to the stage where all the Northants players congregate on the balcony to watch the contest. I had my revenge twice last year with the slower ball and it nearly worked again today, but I just missed his off stump. Then he crashed me a couple of times through the covers, and I think the contest ended in a draw. Personal duels like that evolve over the years. Ned and I are good friends. We enjoy a laugh together and have the highest regard for each other's ability. But it has got to the stage now, largely because of everyone talking about it, that he feels that he has to destroy me from the first ball, and I have to get him out for less than 20.

LARKINS ABOUT: Ned on the attack.

David Munden

29 April

Northamptonshire 176 and 17 for 1
Leicestershire 327 all out: De Freitas 66; Briers 63; Agnew 38

Another good day, with victory in sight. But it needed a rearguard action to build our lead, and Daffy in particular played really well. I went out to bat at 270 for eight just as the fielders' heads were dropping, and the bowlers were feeling every ache and pain. I played a few shots and rode my luck, and should have got a fifty, but I had a rush of blood and holed out at long on. There were plenty of laughs on the pitch, with Allan Lamb trying to put me off. He kept going on about turkeys. My father is a poultry farmer, and supplies several players at Christmas. Lamby kept going on about turkey rustlers and whether my father had started rearing the turkeys for next Christmas or not. It made it very hard to concentrate. My departure brought Les to the crease. There appears to have been some trouble between him and Winston Davis in the past, because Davis bowled him five consecutive bouncers. Les was upset and resorted to patting down the wicket right up at Davis's end to emphasise his point. The result was more bouncers next over. Although it is very funny watching from the safety of the dressing room, I know from experience that it is really frightening for a tail end batsman to be subjected to that sort of barrage. Recognised batters do not understand what it is like to not see a bouncer until the ball is a couple of feet away from your head. It is terrifying. Umpires must stop that sort of attack, but today they did nothing. Les did not last long afterwards. He had a mow at Nick Cook, and holed out.

Our "Anfield" sign arrived today, and was stuck up above the stairs in the pavilion. It has a picture of a running fox, with Leicestershire CCC underneath it. The Northants lads spotted it immediately, and even worked out why it was there. It raised a few laughs from the likes of Nick Cook and Allan Lamb — not what it was designed for.

30 April

Northamptonshire 176 and 100 all out: De Freitas 5 for 40; Agnew 5 for 56
Leicestershire 327
Leicestershire won by an innings and 51 runs

"Selector nudging" is how Pat Murphy termed it in an interview after the match. I had to agree. Match figures of 11 for 122 is, I think, a career best. The only chance I had of making the England side this summer was to start with a bang, and that has happened. Even so, I could have bowled better this match, but luck was on my side. The Northants batsmen must be bitterly disappointed by their inept display. But who cares? It is performances that get recognised.

I am delighted for Daffy. He bowled tremendously again today, and he needs the wickets almost as badly as I do. I am sure he will start off in the Internationals now, but he is not guaranteed a spot in the Test Matches. He is not trying to bowl too fast at the moment, but just letting the ball do the work. That is how he has always done well for us. Mike Gatting seems to have this thing about racing in and ripping peoples' heads off, and that has affected Daffy when he has played for England.

Poor old Les is far from happy. He bowled only two overs in the whole match, and is struggling. He feels that he is only a stop gap until George Ferris is fit again after breaking his ankle, and he desperately wants to prove that he is not over the hill. He cannot prove anything while he is standing down on the fine leg boundary and people are starting to make little jokes about it. Someone said "well bowled Les" today when he did not bowl a ball.

Generally morale is very high. We believe we can clean up this summer. We will back our pace attack against any in the country, and so will carry on producing helpful wickets. Naturally I am pleased, but there could be some reaction from Lord's about the early finishes around the country. Four-day matches were introduced to encourage the batsmen to build big innings and too many have finished inside the distance. But you must prepare pitches to suit your own side. It would be crazy to make a feather bed at Grace Road, just so all the batsmen can score a heap of runs and bowling a side out twice becomes impossible.

CHAPTER THREE

Hot Tempers, Sweaty Betty

1 May

Refuge Assurance League

Leicestershire 173 for 8: Agnew 16
Northamponshire 112 all out: Taylor 3 for 20; Agnew 3 for 32
Leicestershire won by 61 runs

We finished our demolition job on Northants with an excellent victory. Again our batsmen had their Sunday problems, but the tailenders all chipped in and it looked as if the Northants batsmen did not fancy it at all. The pitch was green again, with a bit of bounce, but it was the same story as in the past three days — we played much better in every department.

Les got some wickets thank goodness, but I think his days may be numbered. George Ferris played his first game and got the first two wickets. He can bowl very fast indeed, and had a good season last year, but he has had a lot of injury problems. He is not fully fit yet after breaking a bone in his ankle during the winter. If he is fit he will play because of his extra pace. It might cause problems with the new ball though. Today he and Daffy took it, and I did not say anything as it was a limited overs job. But I would expect to open the bowling in a three or four day match. I am the only swing bowler, and need the new ball.

Everyone seemed happy, and so they should be. Most of the bowlers have taken wickets now, and of the batsmen only Gower has yet to score a fifty. However there are still those worries and problems of last year lurking just beneath the surface, and it only takes a moment of tension or aggression to bring them out.

47

2 May

A day full of drama as we headed for Scotland for tomorrow's Benson and Hedges match. It began at East Midlands Airport when Sid, our second team scorer, set off the security alarm as he checked in. Security staff were scampering everywhere, converging on poor old Sid, who calmly said: "Don't panic. This always happens." He peeled up his trousers to reveal an artificial leg! Crisis over.... until we were within sight of our destination. I am mad on flying and I got permission to sit in the cockpit for the final leg of the flight. As we came in to land, about five hundred feet up, we heard on our radio the pilot of the plane ahead tell the control tower that he had blown both his tyres. The runway was blocked. Immediately we had to abort our landing which was very dramatic. The pilot and co pilot had their hands full throwing switches, and getting us into a steep climb. One hour and twenty minutes later after countless circuits over the airport, we eventually touched down. I thoroughly enjoyed it, but it was not so riveting for the lads in the back of the plane. George Ferris and Les are both bad flyers, and had to be virtually pushed on board at East Midlands. They panicked when we lurched out of our approach and climbed almost vertically. With rain lashing against the windows, it was obvious that we will struggle to play tomorrow, and so the on-board bar got a bashing.

By the time we got out of the airport it was midnight and taxis were hard to find. There we were, seventeen of us with all our kit standing outside in the pouring rain. The mood was ugly.

3 May

Benson and Hedges Cup

Scotland v Leicestershire
No play. Rain

The most common question I am asked is "What do you do when it rains?". Today it was put to me several times and for good reason. We heard at breakfast from umpire Jack Birkenshaw that there would be no play before lunch, and it was unlikely all day. He made an early morning recce of the ground and said it was like a marsh and that there was hardly anything in the way of covering. The first objective was to fill between nine o'clock and lunchtime. Our regular card school of myself, Willey, Taylor and Whitticase got together. We only play the game, Sweaty Betty. It may not be the most mentally stimulating of games, but it is entertaining. Will, usually one of the better players, kept losing and we thoroughly enjoyed his anguish.

Then it was back to the chaos, as we piled into the taxis again, complete with all our kit. Birky was right. I do not think I have ever seen a wetter cricket field. I walked out to the middle and the water sloshed over my shoes. It will be a miracle if we play tomorrow. We would rather not play at all than face a ten overs slog, because that evens up the contest. It only takes Clive Rice to go beserk with the bat and the pressure would really be on.

Our return flight is not until eleven o'clock tomorrow night, and we have to be out of our hotel rooms by midday. If there is no play tomorrow some of the lads are muttering about catching the train home, and others about hiring a car. As usual the one who seems keenest to go is Peter Willey. He has to be the first at everything; the first to get into a taxi, the first down for breakfast, and the first to bat in the nets.

We spent the afternoon clothes shopping for Les. Daffy has decided he is too old fashioned, and needs a trendy image for his Benefit next year. Les tried on all sorts of technicolour baggy trousers, or rods as he calls them, and eventually invested in a couple of pairs, with baggy shirts to match. He needs a good excuse for Our Sue, who controls the purse strings in the Taylor household. She will be far from impressed at Les blowing all his expenses. He decided he would wear one of his outfits for dinner this evening, but needed Daffy and Phil Whitticase in our room to dress him. They tried to persuade him to put some gel in his hair too, but he drew the line at that! Eventually dressed in blue baggies, stone shirt and a blue with white diamonds tie, Les strutted into the hotel bar. The first person to spot him unfortunately was Willey. "Mutton dressed as bloody lamb!"

Les, my "roomie", has just said: "It's bloody rodding down over the Clyde". Roughly translated: "It is raining heavily outside". I do not think we have a hope of playing tomorrow.

4 May

Scotland v Leicestershire
Match abandoned

The match was abandoned without a ball being bowled at nine o'clock this morning. We did not even bother going to the ground. We switched to an early flight and got home to find it pouring in Leicester, too. A fruitless trip. Pure frustration. Gloom for tomorrow.

5 May

Britannic Assurance County Championship
Kent 121 all out: Taylor 67 not out; Agnew 6 for 37
Leicestershire 12 for 0

49

Today I was not given the new ball. It was the first time that has happened for years except when I was not fully fit and I am still seething. I was shattered and mystified when Gower told me. I took over one hundred wickets last year opening the bowling, and have just taken eleven against Northants. My confidence was sky high. Gower did not even tell me tactfully. While loosening up before going onto the field, I said: "Do we know who's opening the batting for them?" Gower said: "Yes, but do we know who is opening for us?" with a smile all over his face. "We'll have George and Daffy." I could not believe it, and just sat in my seat. Then he called me over to have a chat. He said George had to open because of his extra pace, which is fair enough. But I am the only swing bowler in the team, and rely on the new ball. I do not believe that he realised what he had done, and what a shattering effect it would have on me. I began to protest, but we had to go on the field, so I slunk off to fine leg and sulked.

The other players were terrific. They all knew that I had been stuffed, and they all knew why too. It was because Gower was too scared to take the new ball from Daffy. Last year, Ferris and I opened, and had a great partnership. In the background was all the trouble surrounding Daffy, and it is obvious that Gower does not want to upset him. At tea, after I had bowled just one over, we had another chat in the physio's room. Gower said: "Before you start, remember that whenever you bowl, you are still a fine bowler."

I said: "Look at it from a batters point of view. Say you are an opening bat who scored two thousand runs last year, and started this season with a double hundred. Then you were told that you were being relegated to number seven. How would you feel?" He shrugged his shoulders. I was close to tears through sheer frustration. When play resumed I was bowling one end, and between sulks at fine leg I ripped Kent's batting apart. I proved a point.

My team mates were great in encouraging me, because they could see how upset I was and Gower had the grace to say "well bowled" afterwards. OK. I took six for 37. It was the perfect reply, but it did nothing to help my temper.

Mike Turner was not there, but I will make sure that I have a chat with him tomorrow about the new ball. What happened today is the nearest thing to being dropped from the team.

6 May

Kent 121 and 17 for 3
Leicestershire 296 all out: Boon 131; De Freitas 60; Alleyne 5 for 54

I got to the ground early this morning, but not as early as the Kent lads. They were on jankers, and had to be outside loosening up at 9.30. That is always the first sign of a captain's frustration at his team's poor performance, and Chris Cowdrey obviously felt that yesterday's batting display warranted some sort of positive action. I was there to see Mike Turner. He had watched the closing stages of yesterday's play. He could plainly see that I was not happy, and had guessed why. He said he would have a word with Gower, and then we all could talk about it openly.

Gower called me into the physio's room while I was waiting to bat, and Nigel Briers joined us too. Gower explained again his reasons for me not opening. He believed that I could adapt best to not having the new ball. He said that I would bowl after George, who normally burns himself out after seven or eight overs. Nigel backed him up, so I could see that I was not going to get anywhere.

That was it, and I went out to bat. I was crippled by a Hartley Alleyne thunderbolt, which went right through my pad, and he then bounced me out with a ''rib tickler''. One for the little black book!

Then, surprise, surprise, Gower announced that I would be opening the bowling with George. Again I proved my point by taking two wickets, and George took one to set up victory tomorrow.

Tim Boon batted superbly well for his century. It was a real hard graft. When he came off the pitch at tea with just over 100 to his name, we all said well played, and then brought him down to earth by showing him Teletext.

G. Hick ... not out 405.

7 May

Kent 121 and 128 all out: De Freitas 4 for 52; Agnew 3 for 45
Leicestershire 296 all out: Boon 131; Agnew 2
Leicestershire won by an innings and 47 runs

Another thrashing of a visiting side at Grace Road. Daffy bowled with a lot of venom on a wicket which was hardly doing a thing. After the match Chris Cowdrey said that he felt his side had been beaten by this year's County champions. High praise indeed. In the dressing room afterwards we were all saying: ''Right, who's next?'' and not caring at all who it is. We feel we can beat anyone.

Spent the evening with Richard Ellison and some of the lads watching Steve Davis beat Leicester's Willie Thorne in the Rothman's Matchroom Snooker League. I had a word with Davis, and I asked if he had problems motivating himself on that sort of occasion, given that just over a week ago he was winning the World Championship. He said that in principle, motivation is straightforward. He wakes up in the morning, takes stock of what is on that day, and prepares himself accordingly. I was amazed at the set up this evening. The whole thing was centred around money. You could almost smell it. The MC made sure that everybody who had sponsored the slightest thing got a mention at some stage, usually with some corny slogan. But it seems to work. The money those fellows get is unbelievable.

We sat there whispering and joking amongst ourselves, wondering when Willie Thorne was last forced to go on a gruelling training run, or if Steve Davis has ever felt how we do when a psychopathic West Indian fast bowler is running in to bowl at us, intent on nothing less than decapitation. Nevertheless it was a pleasure and a privilege to watch Davis in action. He played a couple of sensational shots, and ran out the winner by five frames to three. A couple more victories in that league, and he earns another £70,000. I think that is more than I have earned in ten years of professional cricket.

8 May

Refuge Assurance League

Leicestershire v Kent
Match abandoned. Rain

Abandoned before lunch after a monsoon during the night. We are now off until Thursday, when we face Warwickshire in the Benson and Hedges Cup. Daffy signed a new two-year contract over the weekend. Last year he seemed determined to leave us, but he seems happy now and must have done enough to be picked for the One Day Internationals.

The newspaper *Today* has accepted my first offering and I hope to be writing for them on a regular basis. With the cricket going well, I am plucking up the coverage to tell Radio Leicester that I will not be joining them this winter.

12 May

Benson and Hedges Cup
Leicestershire 196 for 9: Gower 53; Agnew 3; Merrick 4 for 24
Warwickshire 187 all out: Kallicharan 79; Ferris 5 for 28; Agnew 1 for 49
Leicestershire won by 9 runs

A sensational win. "Quality shovelling" was the concensus in the dressing room afterwards. We should never have won the match, but we kept applying the pressure to their batsmen, and they cracked. My first three overs probably blew any chance I might have had of being picked for the One Day Internationals. With Micky Stewart watching, I bowled dreadfully. I had no rhythm, and my first three overs went for 17 runs. I can put it down to a bad day at the office, but of all days to pick ... I came back and bowled well at Kallicharan but Micky Stewart had seen enough by then and had gone. George and Daffy bowled well, and got me off the hook. The final overs were really tense, especially when Tony Merrick slogged Ferris for a four to bring it down to less than ten required. George got his revenge by splattering his stumps all over the place, and then did some sort of war dance in delight. He is a lovely character and the crowd at Grace Road has really taken to him. For a mean fast bowler he behaves almost comically on the field, with outrageous appeals for lbw followed by a sheepish apology to the umpire. There is not an ounce of malice in George. He is deeply religous, and is often to be seen quietly in prayer in the dressing room. He once went slightly over the top during a particularly aggressive match with Middlesex in which there had been a lot of short pitched bowling, and George had smashed Roland Butcher's cheekbone. It came to George's turn to bat against Cowans and Daniel, eager to seek retribution for their mate who was still in hospital suffering from concussion.

"Please God, don't let them kill me," he implored as he left the dressing room. And poor old George meant it. He has not reproduced the kind of pace he had since inflicting that damage on Butcher. It affected George deeply. He was the Man of The Match today, and rightly so. He even saluted the crowd with the medal, F.A.Cup style. The talk afterwards was all about Martin, and the effect he has had on us. There is no doubt that he helped us win today. The word "shovel" was never actually used, but it did not need to be. Whenever anyone clapped their hands and shouted "Come on lads" it raised everyone. Warwickshire lost the game because we bowled well after the first 10 overs, and they cracked under the pressure.

13 May

We arrived at the ground expecting a practise on yesterday's pitch but instead we were presented with green, damp nets to bowl on. I blew up at Higgy. After a few minutes it was obvious we were wasting our time. Les nearly ripped Willey's thumb off with a ball that flew off a length. The groundsman was then summoned, and he reluctantly put a net around the wicket as we originally wanted.

At last I have got my run up sorted out. I feel much more relaxed running in now, and I bowled fast just by adding a couple of paces on. My rhythm was back, and I swung the ball. It was not Willey's day. Having survived the blow on the thumb, he had a knock on the pitch, and I ripped one back into his inside thigh. He was hopping about, swearing and cursing much to our amusement. But he may be struggling for tomorrow which will be a massive blow. We have to beat Derby to be sure of qualifying for the next stage of the competition. We need Will to play.

I hope I will be picked. With Les breathing down our necks, one bad

THAT'S OUT ... SURELY: George's 'mean' look.

Graham Morris

performance might be enough. I hope I do not have nightmares tonight. We are back at The Racecourse Ground tomorrow. I wonder what state the showers are in.

14 May

Benson and Hedges Cup

Leicestershire 186 for 5: De Freitas 57
Derbyshire 190 for 4: Barnett 71; Bowler 55; Agnew 0 for 22
Derbyshire won by 6 wickets

We are out of the Benson And Hedges Cup, mainly because our match against Scotland was abandoned. Our run rate was not as good as Warwickshire's who scored 300 against them, and so Warwicks go through, even though we beat them on Thursday. We lost today but only just, and it left a feeling of deep depression after the match. We so nearly pulled this one off. We were always a good thirty runs short of a decent target, and only a typically aggressive knock from Daffy gave us anything to bowl at.

The day started with a phone call from Mike Gatting. "Sorry mate, you've not made it, but we gave you a lot of thought. We've decided to stick with the old brigade. Keep going."

I appreciated the call. I have always got on well with Gatt, and would like to play under him. It is certainly an interesting side. No Gower, and no Botham. Pringle in despite a nightmare in the World Cup, and a debut for Monte Lynch. His selection has caused an uproar in our dressing room. It is not because he is not a good player but because he has already played for the rebel West Indians in South Africa. How on earth can someone who had represented another country be picked to play for England? Peter Willey in particular feels very strongly about it. He even picked an alternative England team for Daffy to give to Gatt on Wednesday. It read, in batting order:

Gehan Mendis
Wilf Slack
Graeme Hick
Roland Butcher
Robin Smith
Rodney Ontong
Jack Russell: (he could not think of a foreign English keeper)
Kevin Curran
Neil Williams
Alan Warner
Devon Malcolm

56

Not a bad side, but Will has a point.

Gower seemed quite realistic about his situation. "It's a long summer," was his reaction. At least we will have him for Wednesday's match against Middlesex, who have been decimated. No Gatting, no Emburey and no Downton. That is quite a chunk out of their batting line up, and we will back ourselves to beat them.

Back to today's match. It was when they were about 80 without loss off 25 overs the Will turned to me and said: "Forget the shovel, we need a bloody J.C.B.!" As I made my way to fine leg in front of the pavilion, I caught Tim Boon's eye inside our dressing room. He had been forced to retire hurt after being hit on the left arm by a Devon Malcolm missile. He had just returned from hospital, and the look on his face now said it all. His arm was broken, and he would be out for three months. What can you say? Especially to a guy who missed 1986 because of a broken leg, and then missed much of 1987 with a broken finger. "Bad luck" cannot begin to sum up how we feel for him. All his hopes and ambitions for the season are forgotten. We could not work out why he had not worn his arm guard, which is basically a shin pad strapped to the forearm. "I don't know. It was the first time that I have not worn it", he said. That piece of protection was lying in his kit bag all along, and would have prevented the bone from breaking. Why on earth did he not put it on, as he always did before every innings this year?

Derbyshire so nearly blew it. Peter Bowler scored 50 in as many overs, and there was terrible pressure on the batsmen who came in after him. They wanted about 20 off the final three overs, when Bruce Roberts edged two leg side boundaries off De Freitas, and then Michael Holding edged two fours past the keeper off George. There is nothing you can do about that. It is pure luck, and it cost us the match.

17 May

Bertha's replacement arrived today by special carrier. A magnificent three pound weapon fresh from Duncan Fearnley's warehouse. It is called The Rapier and has a pair of flashing swords on the blade. Apparently Graeme Hick uses one. That cannot be a bad recommendation. His single innings of 405 the other day is more than I scored all last season! Gower has doctored the face of the bat so it now reads "The Raper". I had a net with her this morning, and certainly assaulted Peter Willey's bowling a couple of times. She is much heavier than the late Bertha, so I will have to have some more practice tomorrow before unleashing her on the formidable Middlesex attack, which still, thankfully, is without Wayne Daniel.

He and I have the original love/hate relationship. We get on like a house on fire off the pitch, but on it we are like cat and dog. It started way back in 1981, when we played Middlesex at Lord's. He had just taken the second

57

THE GRIM RAPER: Agnew at the ready.

David Munden

new ball as I strode to the wicket, with Leicestershire in a very strong position. He bowled like a maniac. Round the wicket and everything pitched in his own half. In the end I was taking a large step to leg, and trying to smash anything I could reach. Mike Brearley then got in on the act by setting the field with everyone on the off side. It was a farce, and seemed to set the trend for whenever we meet. He tries to rip my head off, I try to do the same to him, and then we go to the pub and buy each other a drink. I would be very happy if our hostilities were to cease. Mercifully he did something serious to his back early in the season, and is only set to return to action on the weekend against Cambridge. Poor students. They will not know what hit them. A rampaging Wayne Daniel trying to prove his fitness!

Today I turned my back on the BBC. There is no way that I could give up cricket now. Things are going too well on the field, and there is the prospect of a future at Leicestershire off the field too.

I have been offered a job as Cricket Development Officer, organising, coaching at junior and youths levels and developing Kwik Cricket in primary schools. Mike Turner also told me there could be a future for me in cricket administration, and that I could become more involved in that side of things in coming winters. I am delighted. I now have security and I can also stay in the game.

18 May

Britannic Assurance County Championship
Leicestershire 114 all out: Cobb 31; Agnew 3 not out; Williams 5 for 46
Middlesex 212 for 1: Carr 136 not out; Brown 58

"A complete nightmare. We batted, bowled and fielded like idiots. Let's pick ourselves up, and make sure this is the only bad day of the season." Gower's words during our first collective bollocking. We throughly deserved it too. The wicket was very slow, and the ball only moved about a fraction. But our batting was pathetic. We lost our last six wickets for only ten runs in the space of five overs. Nobody really got in and grafted which is what the situation demanded. Then John Carr came in and played one of the best innings I have seen for some time. He smashed the ball everywhere. He was in a bad trot, and decided that he would hit his way out of it. Unfortunately, he had to pick on us.

The Middlesex innings got off to an amazing start. I was about to run in and bowl at Wilf Slack when he suddenly keeled over at the crease. I thought he had had a heart attack and died. His eyes were wide open, and he was staring straight down at the wicket, unconscious.

Our lads rushed up to him to see what was wrong, but I could not. Wilf is a good mate of mine; we roomed together on tour, and I believed that he was dead. One of his legs was twitching, and Peter Willey was groping in his mouth, making sure he had not swallowed his tongue. After what seemed like an age Wilf started to move, and came round. As he sat up, I walked down and said "Bad luck mate. While you were unconscious I've knocked your middle pole out! You're out!"

Wilf laughed, and wanted to carry on batting. We told him to forget it, and he walked off the field as if nothing had happened. The incident left us shaken. There was no doctor on the ground, and this proved that one must be in attendance at all times. Craig was busy treating someone in his room, and so did not see what happened, but that is beside the point. He is a physio not a doctor. We have all had training in artificial respiration, but I know that I froze today when we were confronted with a real situation.

One day there could well be a tragedy. Cricket is a potentially lethal game with a rock-hard ball being propelled at speeds of up to 90 miles per hour. A batsman has only two fifths of a second to react and play a shot to a ball from a fast bowler. Think about it. People are bound to get hurt.

Soon after that Phil Whitticase missed a ball behind the stumps from Chris Lewis and with a horrible crack it hit him straight between his eyes. There was a lot of blood. He was concussed and left the field. James Whitaker reluctantly took over as wicket keeper, and promptly dropped Carr who was on 90 at the time. He then missed a throw from the boundary which went for four overthrows. Finally he threw the gloves away in disgust and Chris Lewis had a go. He did well. Once again we had to wait for five overs before we could have a sub on the field. That rule is ridiculous.

19 May

Leicestershire 114 and 201 for 4: Gower 74
Middlesex 329 all out: Carr 144; Agnew 6 for 67

That was the performance I needed. That is my third six-wicket haul this year, and I now have 31 first class wickets. Today I felt right too. My rhythm was good and I bowled well. I know England's seamers did a good job in the first One Day International, but the selectors said that team was picked on merit after one-day performances. I hope that the Test team will be picked on performances in the County Championship

We are still in a desperate position in this match. The only good thing today was Gower getting runs at last. His first twenty were very scratchy, and he looked very depressed and out of sorts with himself. But gradually his timing came back, and he played some beautiful strokes. When he got out, he was furious. Clearly a good sign, as he desperately wanted a century.

Peter Willey was out for a duck, which took him half an hour. He is still hopelessly out of touch, and it is getting to him. He is starting to get aggressive with me, disagreeing with everything I say, and generally winding me up. It is a defensive mechanism, as usually we are the best of friends. But I hope he scores some runs soon!

I had a difference of opinion with *Today* when a reporter phoned for a quote on why I thought Graeme Hick should be able to play for England immediately. The paper is running a 'Hick for England" campaign. I told him I was totally opposed it and asked if I could give the professional cricketer's view in my next article. No chance, they said. I feel very strongly about Hick and the others who have actually got into the England side. I do not understand how they can feel any kind of loyalty to England. They are not English, and that is it. Just because Hick is a brilliant player is no reason to make him a special case. You are either born English or you are not. Virtually every professional cricketer would back me up on that.

20 May

Leicestershire 114 and 265: Whitaker 55; Potter 39 not out; Agnew 1; Williams 4 for 60
Middlesex 329 and 52 for 2: Agnew 0-2
Middlesex won by 8 wickets

I formally resigned from the BBC, after we had taken more stick from Middlesex. The former left me with a feeling of relief. It had been hanging over me like a black cloud for some days. The latter was humiliating. Everyone was numb afterwards as we sat in silence in the dressing room. No one said anything. Not even Gower. He did not have to. He had said it all on Wednesday evening. It is important to realise at times like this that it is not the end of the world, and there has to be a loser. Fortunately with professional cricket, the next game is the following day, and so heavy defeats are quickly forgotten. It must be awful being a footballer having suffered an 8-0 defeat, and having to wait a week before playing again. We have another important game tomorrow, and it sounds as If Ian Botham will not be playing. It should be another lively wicket, so we should pick ourselves up very quickly if we win the toss.

21 May

Britannic Assurance County Championship
Worcestershire 286 for 7: Neale 77; Curtis 57

The pitch we hoped would be a minefield turned out to be more like a blamange. Worcestershire are without their top three bowlers, so we really wanted a seamer's paradise, just like the other wickets we have had here this summer. For some reason this one is brown, and the ball has done nothing. The pitch is very slow, which accounts for the the low score. It is ironic that after all that has been written and said about the pitches here at Grace Road that when we really wanted a rough one it should turn out to be as flat as this.

I bowled my best spell of the year without taking a wicket. I never even felt that I would. Gower did the dirty on me this evening. I had not bowled for an hour, and Les had been on from my end. There was one over to go from that end before the close of play, and Gower suddenly told me to get loose, and bowl it. I thought he was winding me up, because I had bowled thirty overs already, and was really stiff. But no, he meant it, and I had to bowl. I gave Les a filthy look as I strode past him at mid on. He thought the whole thing was hilarious of course, and I could see him killing himself laughing as I ran in looking like a man riddled with rigor mortis. He made up for it by buying me a drink afterwards.

It was a disappointing day. We had hoped for so much, especially when it was confirmed that Botham would not be playing. We have let a golden opportunity slip past here. I hope we will not look back on this game in the middle of September and say "If only."

22 May

Refuge Assurance League
Leicestershire 197 for 9: Gower 50; Agnew 8 not out; Pridgeon 4 for 36
Worcestershire 201 for 6 39.4 overs: Curtis 50; Hick 66; Agnew 1 for 37
Worcestershire won by 4 wickets

A bloody awful day. The sort you would not wish on your worst enemy. It took me the best part of an hour to drive the four miles to the ground this morning. There was some kind of vintage car rally going on, and Leicester was at a standstill. Eventually I arrived at the ground half an hour late, and in a terrible rage. Worse was to come.

I was loosening up when I spotted Bob "Knocker" White, one of the umpires, bearing down on me. "Sorry Aggers mate. I've pranged your car in the car park. Looks bad." Now Knocker is a hell of a nice guy. One of those umpires who just gets on with the job with no messing about, and is as honest as the day is long. There were at least thirty cars in the car park that morning and I would have had no idea who had hit mine. But he had the decency to come up and tell me. My gleaming white Scirocco. I am so proud of it. The lads know that, and so there was a fair bit of mickey taking in the nets. Afterwards I plucked up courage to go and have an inspection. It looked a real mess. All the rear side panel was caved in.

Suddenly there was a bit of a fracas in the Worcester dressing room. The match was underway, and as they were fielding, there were only a couple of their lads on the balcony. A man had got through the security on the pavilion door, gone into their dressing room and started to get changed into whites. Gordon Lord, their twelfth man, spotted him, and asked him what he was doing.

"I'm Typhoon Tim. I'm ever so sorry I'm late. I'm playing for you today. How long will it before the skipper needs me?" was the reply.

The Police were called and gently led Typhoon away. Apparently he had come in with a proper cricket case, and told the attendant at the pavilion door that he was a player. The old boy believed him. Gordon Lord summed it up. Typhoon was judged to be "a couple of sandwiches short of a full picnic!'"

The game was another typical Leicestershire Sunday performance. I found myself batting with five overs still to go, and George and I had to make sure that we used every ball. George was thrilled when he hit the last ball out of the ground for a massive six, but that was the last smile on anyone's face, as Graeme Hick showed everyone what a magnificent player he is. He tore our bowling to shreds. I had really fancied us to win the match, but he cut loose with eight an over needed, and although he got out with ten runs still required, he had done his bit. I have never seen anyone hit the ball so hard. At one point I was fielding at very close fine leg to George. I was there because he wanted his mid off back on the fence, which meant that he needed another fielder inside the circle. It is an awful spot. You get about half a second to see the ball, which flies off the edge at about ninety miles an hour. Hick flicked two past me, both of which he had taken from ouside off stump. As George kept saying afterwards: "Man, dere's nothing you can do about dat!"

Worcestershire have the rowdiest supporters on the circuit. They are a pain in the neck for the average cricket spectator, and the players too for that matter. They scream and chant endlessly from the boundary edge, and generate an atmosphere of real aggression. They invaded our pub *The Cricketers* last night too. I like going in there for a quick drink after a long day, but it was full of morons shouting and jeering. I slipped over to a table in the corner with Gordon Parsons, who had been dropped from the Warwickshire team for the day, and I was consoling him when a drunken young fellow stumbled over to our table asking for an autograph. I recognised him by the very smart Duncan Fearnley bag he was clutching. It was none other than Typhoon Tim.

23 May

Worcestershire 291 and 32 for 4: Ferris 5 for 47; Agnew 0 for 73
Leicestershire 280 for 5 dec.: Whitaker 100 not out

We are in a great position to win this match. It took a bold declaration by David Gower who decided to gamble our fourth batting point for a crack at their batsmen, and it paid off. I got a couple of wickets, George got one, and then Laurie Potter struck when it became too dark for George and I to bowl. If we can get at Graeme Hick early tomorrow, we should sew it up. He has pulled a thigh muscle, and so was unable to bat this evening.

I gave Mike Garnham a lift home afterwards. He retired two years ago, and is only playing this game because Whitticase still has two black eyes. At the time, Mike was convinced that he was doing the right thing. He was disillusioned with professional cricket. He did not like the internal wranglings, and did not get on with Peter Willey.

At his best he was brilliant. He took a superb diving catch down the leg side off me today. But he was always outspoken and often got into trouble with club. He ended up getting fined and banned during his last season. Les reckoned they had only asked Mike to play in this match because they were a bit short of cash, and needed to fine him again!

Mike told me how much he had enjoyed the past few days. There was no pressure on him, and he agreed that he had missed the big time. I would not be surprised if he makes a comeback elsewhere. It was reassuring to hear him say he had missed the game. I know I would.

May 24

Worcestershire 291 and 222 for 7 dec.: Curtis 78; Illingworth 60; Agnew 2 for 36
Leicestershire 280 for 5 and 99 for 5
Match Drawn

Today we got details of next week's trip to Holland and Les is far from happy. He is only going if Daffy is playing in the first Test, and feels very left out. It was done rather insensitively. The list was simply stuck up on the board, and read De Freitas/Taylor. After thirteen years with the club Les thought that he deserved to go on the trip. It is only a social affair after all.

I am sure Daffy will be picked for England anyway, but Les is now threatening to feign an injury, and not go. It is all a bit stupid. We are playing four friendly matches on matting wickets. They tend to be lethal if fast bowlers put in too much effort, and so the whole trip is really a bit of fun, and a way of passing off an empty week. Tim Boon is going, though, which is a good gesture by the club.

The worst aspect of the trip is that we are being billeted out, which can easily ruin a tour. It all depends on your hosts. Some are great, they simply let you come and go as you please. Others are too kind. They fuss all over you, prepare a meal every night so you can't go out, and organise every spare minute of your day. It sounds ungrateful, but I am sure everyone knows what I mean.

That is all a week away. Today's match was a terrible disappointment. We just seemed to drift along this morning without inspiration when we were trying to bowl Worcester out. In the end we almost lost the game halfheartedly chasing 234 to win. There was a howling gale blowing straight down the hill, and Chris was overbowled again. He battled away for an hour and a half into the hurricane, and that is far too much for a twenty year old. He is begining to show signs of fatigue now, struggling to the crease and bowling too many loose deliveries. I have spent time encouraging him, and he is keen to learn. It makes a change to have one of the younger lads listening to advice. They seem to know it all. Chris is very talented, and worth the effort. But he needs a rest.

Peter Such tried desperately hard to get out of the second team's match against Middlesex. Rumours were flying that Wayne Daniel is due to make his comeback, after failing to play against the students. Such relishes batting against Wayne about as much as I do, and seems to have taken a leaf out of Whitticase's book. He suddenly appeared in Craig's room with a terrible black eye, hit while supervising the second team's fielding practice. Guy Lovell, a left arm spinner nicknamed Clyde because his movements in the field closely resemble the Orang Utang in *Any Which Way But Loose*, had thrown a ball in and hit Suchy flush in the face. There was a whisper that with the possibility of fending off Daniel, Suchy dived in the way of the ball

We are now third in the Championship behind Middlesex and Worcestershire. We would have settled for that at the start of the season, but again we now have three days off. I have a niggle in my left ankle caused by a bad foothold and need treatment. On Thursday we have a team session with Martin. We have not seen him since our win over Warwickshire and I feel we need to. I was disappointed by our attitude today. We could have been on top of the table tonight but the fight was not there.

25 May

I know I am setting myself up, but I think I will be picked for the First Test. A couple of Micky Stewart's quotes in the Press today make me feel that I have a good chance. He said the One Day International victories were terrific, but the Tests will be hard, and there will be team changes to suit five-day rather than one-day cricket. Mike Selvey said on Test Match Special that I should play. He reckons that I should be picked before Daffy because I swing the ball away from the bat. I cannot see Daffy being dropped but I could get in instead of Radford. That would make me the fourth seamer, and probable twelfth man. That would not bother me at all. At least it would be a foot in the door.

I went in for treatment this morning and found Daffy was playing for the second team. He asked to play, which is amazing. From a packed Lord's one minute to a deserted Grace Road the next. He reckons he needs some batting practice. I think it shows that he has got the bit between his teeth.

26 May

More treatment on my ankle, and it feels pretty good. But I could not run or bowl because of the weather. Why does it always rain on our days off?

I met Gordon Parsons again at Grace Road. He left Leicestershire three seasons ago for what he hoped would be a rosier career at Warwickshire. But he is struggling to get in the side. He and Warwickshire's new captain, Andy Lloyd, do not seem to see eye to eye. Gordon has always been an aggressive bloke on the field, and it seems Lloyd does not like his tantrums. He cannot even get into the one day side. He and I have always been good mates, in fact he is Jennifer's godfather, and he had a good moan this morning. He came to me for advice when he decided to leave Leicester, and I thought Warwicks would be the best place for him, so I feel slightly responsible. I think deep down he would love to come back to us. With Les at the twilight of his career, there could be an opening for him.

Martin was on good form. Apart from the word "shovel", he has not suggested much, but he is getting us to talk while he listens. Because we all feel so relaxed, out come our worries. And he makes sure that everyone, including the most junior second team member, has his say. Today we talked about the winning habit we had found, and why it has gone now. Why were we winning? What were we doing then that we are not doing now? Do we think that people are playing differently? Are we happy with life? The conclusion was that we are, except with the practice facilities, which have been awful. The batsmen have not been in great nick in the matches because of the green wickets. They go into the nets to get into some sort of form, and they feel even worse. James Whitaker feels particularly strongly about it. He is a keen netter and has to feel totally happy with his form to score runs in the middle. He feels the nets have been working against us. Mike Turner promised things would improve.

There are three distinct groups when it comes to practice once the season is underway. There are the fanatical practicers who live in the nets, and then go and throw balls to each other afterwards. That group comprises of Whitaker, Cobb, Boon, Briers and Potter. The second group includes myself, Les, Daffy, George, Willey and Whitticase. We all enjoy a day off, and only have a really hard practice if we are out of touch, or if we have not played for two or three days. The third group consists of just one man. Our captain. Gower only has a net if he is desperately out of touch. If the net goes badly he plays a host of rash shots and then comes out. He does not bowl, simply because he cannot. It is amazing how one of the most natural batsmen the game has ever had is such a terrible bowler. For such an easy mover he is incredibly unco-ordinated when he comes to delivering the ball. It loops out at a very slow speed, like a non-spinning spinner. Apart from Gower, the two groups are very clearly split between batsmen and bowlers. The batters are the fanatical practisers. They seem obsessed with theories. Theories for playing a fast bouncer. Theories for playing a sharp off spinner, and so on. They discuss various things between themselves, and take the nets very seriously. It amazes me that they still go into the nets even if the ball is flying about everywhere. I refuse to bat if the wickets are bad. It only takes a blow on the inside thigh, and that could mean missing a match. The problem then is that I can go two weeks without picking up a bat, and then go out to face the likes of Sylvester Clarke in a match. Seeing the first few balls is a real problem then. A top batter will never go more than two days without feeling a bat in his hands.

27 May

Telephone calls all day have made me all the more sure that I will be selected for the First Test. The most positive sign came form Mike Turner this morning. He told me that Micky Stewart had given him a call, and had given both David Gower and I "Good mentions". I asked David what he thought that meant. "At least it means we've got one vote out of five," he said. When I got home after light training the phone hardly stopped ringing. Chris Lander of *The Sun* did an interview with me along the lines that I had been picked. He would not have bothered to call me if he was not fairly sure what the form was. Lots of friends also called just to say "good luck."

The selectors meet this afternoon, so I may get a call tonight. I reckon that there are three of us, Neil Radford, Paul Jarvis and myself going for two places. I have easily got the most wickets this year, but Radford may also have the edge as he did nothing wrong in the One Day Internationals. I hope I have not tempted fate. This afternoon I took my England sweaters and blazer to the dry cleaners.

28 May

Britannic Assurance County Championship
Northamptonshire 327 for 8: Capel 75; Lamb 70; Agnew 0 for 86

I knew I should not have played today. I had a splitting headache when I turned up at the ground this morning, and by this evening I had developed full blown 'flu. I felt miserable all day, and after a good opening spell I bowled like a drain. The wicket was emerald green but bounced twice through to the wicketkeeper. In fact the groundsman Ray Bailey did me a treat this morning. I always give hime a lot of stick about the wickets at Northampton. They are slow and produce very boring cricket. And when I walked on to the field first thing he was out there alongside the brownest, flattest pitch I have ever seen.

"Morning, Aggy. I think you'll love this one," he said grinning from ear to ear. I gave him a mouthful as usual, and told him the ground needed blowing up, which it does.

"Well if you don't like that one, I'll move the stumps over here, and you can play on this one." He moved the wickets over to a bright green strip. I had been competely fooled. It turns out that the flat one is for the West Indies in a week's time. I certainly pity their bowlers!

I avoided a Nedding by bowling well early on. Larkins played and missed countless times and in the end resorted to a silly stance with his bat waving everywhere and an inane grin on his face, trying to put me off. He hit me for a couple of fours, and I came off after fourteen overs. It had been a good contest. My head felt awful, and I was beginning to ache all over. At lunch, I told Gower that I was struggling. By the close I was shivering, and pulled out of tomorrow's Sunday League match at Old Trafford.

I got the Doctor out when I got home. "Yes. You've got the flu. Three days in bed."

I could not believe it. If I am picked I may miss the Test. And if I spend three days in bed, I am hardly going to be in good shape for a five-day Test with all the pressure that entails. And after all the hard work of the past couple of years.

29 May

Refuge Assurance League
Lancashire 214 for 7 off: Hayhurst 84; Ferris 4 for 24
Leicestershire 99 for 1 off 22.3 overs: Potter 51
Lancashire won on faster scoring rate

I woke up feeling much better and very excited. Today is the day the Test team is announced. I still have a sore throat and headache, but the shivers have gone. I stayed in bed for most of the morning, and at eleven o'clock the phone rang. Bev answered it downstairs and shouted "It's Micky Stewart for you."

My heart was in my mouth as I picked up the phone by the bed. "Hello Micky. How are you?"

"A lot better than you are by the sound of it. I'm sorry you've got the flu, and the news I've got for you won't make you feel any better either. There is a group of you all competing on level terms, and I'm afraid you've just missed out Aggy. Only just I promise you, but that's the way it is I'm afraid."

I thanked Micky for his call, and wished him all the best for the match. Then I just sank back into my pillow and closed my eyes. Bev came up. She was as choked as I was. When I was left out of the One Day matches Gatt

BAD NEWS TRAVELS FAST: Caller Micky Stewart.   David Munden

said to keep going, I was so close. I took another six wicket haul after that. Again I am the country's leading wicket-taker. Why is it the Selectors do not think I can bowl? There must be a flaw in my temperament or something about the way I bowl which is making them reluctant to give me a crack.

I lay in bed listening to the radio, and then the news came on with the full team. Paul Jarvis and Greg Thomas! Thomas did not seem to be in the frame. Jarvis has taken one five-wicket haul all season. John Culley told me at Northampton that one Selector did not want me in because I have to prove that I can take wickets away from Grace Road. We have only played one game away from there all season, so how is that my fault? And what about the 101 I took last year? Half of those were away from home. Stupid little excuses not to pick me.

30 May

Northamptonshire 327 for 8 dec
Leicestershire 143: Agnew absent ill, and 117 for 2

The papers have had a field day. "Diabolical" "Selectors Shocker" were two of the headlines. They have ripped Peter May to bits. There were his reasons on all the back pages:

"We are rather concerned that a lot of bowlers have taken a lot of wickets on what you would not call perfect pitches."A direct reference to me. I find it all very sad. I do not think I will have a better opportunity. Gladstone Small is bound to be fit for the next one, and Neil Foster cannot be far from playing again either.

31 May

Northamptonshire 327 for 8 and 62 for 6
Leicestershire 143 and 264: Cobb 64; Agnew 23
Match drawn

A rearguard action by our tail saved the game. Northants have not beaten Leicestershire in a first class match since 1976. We were well aware of that today, and it helped. I scored 23, and felt in quite good form. Chris Lewis and George Ferris played well too, and together we frustrated the Northants bowlers and fielders. Often when tailenders are blocking for a draw, there is a lot of verbal abuse flying about, all trying to unsettle them. There was none of that today. I think we all know each other too well but there was a lot of short pitched bowling delivered at me in particular. The main offender was David Capel but fortunately the wicket was slow enough for me to cope without too much discomfort. It is strange how my batting form comes and goes. I cannot remember when I last played a proper innings, and I have not had a net for ages. The Raper felt much better. It is heavier than Bertha.

An old mate Robin Jackman, the former Surrey and England bowler, turned up unexpectedly. He is in the country to commentate for the BBC on the first three Tests. We go back to my early days at The Oval when I was a youngster and he was a very senior player. We have always got on well together, and shared a laugh or two this afternoon, with my batting bearing the brunt of his jibes.

The game had an exciting climax with Northants chasing 81 to win from eight overs. They gave it a full thrash, and played some great shots but it was always too much for them. My great regret was that I did not see my hero, Dennis Lillee, bowl a ball. He has severly damaged his ankle, and looks set to miss the rest of the season. What a shame. I would love to have had the chance to have talked to him about bowling, or at least seen him in action.

Holland tomorrow, and a dawn start.

ARRESTING SIGHT: Leslie Brian Taylor.

Graham Morris

CHAPTER FOUR

Innocents Abroad

We could see that there was something wrong when Les's car appeared in the car park at Grace Road. It was a quarter to six in the morning. Most of us were on board the bus, but Les had a very sheepish look on his face.

"I've lost my passport" he explained to a frantic Mike Turner, who was already in a state because Chris Lewis had discovered that his passport was in London. He was flying out the following day. We were quickly losing men! Les was despatched to go and have another search and to join us at East Midlands Airport if he could. If not he was to get a temporary one, and fly out with Lewis. There was a buzz of excitement on the bus, like a schoolboys' outing. Most of us had never been to Holland before, and after all, the cricket was hardly going to be serious. We felt that we were in for a good time.

Les duly arrived at the airport just in time clutching his passport.

"God knows what Our Sue's going to say. I've tipped everything out of every drawer to find this bloody thing, and haven't had time to put it all back. It'll take her days to sort that lot out!" At least he was relieved to have found it. But it was to prove an enormous mistake.

Les is a very straightforward soul. He is a man of the country. He loves going shooting and ferreting, and is the only one of us to live out in the sticks, in a little village near Earl Shilton. He is a great teller of stories with a sense of humour to match, but he calls a spade a spade. He has led a simple life. He was a miner until his bowling talents were spotted in the local league, and he became a professional cricketer. Taking all this into account, he is not the sort of man you would expect to be arrested and charged by Immigration Officials at Schiphol Airport, Amsterdam. But he was.

Poor Les. He has trouble hearing properly spoken English at the best of times. When the Immigration Officer stopped him, and started to question

73

him in a thick Dutch accent, Les had real problems. He could see the rest of use safely through the barrier waving at him, and at first he thought the whole thing was a put up job. But his opinion quickly changed when he was whisked away between two armed men. Mike Turner went to investigate, to be told that there was an irregularity with Les's passport and that he was in serious trouble.

We had to leave Les there. It was ten o'clock, and we were due to play our first match in The Hague at twelve. We were all killing ourselves laughing at poor old Les's predicament. Of all the people it could happen to, it would have to be him.

We were taken to the ground from Schiphol. It was a very English looking club, but the pitch was a form of matting. I had not realised that it was a festival, but in the clubhouse were Don Wilson, John Spencer, Richard Doughty and several other familiar faces from the MCC. They assured me that the whole thing revolved around socialising, and was basically a PR exercise. There are four teams involved playing in a round robin. Us, The MCC, the Dutch equivilent called The Flamingoes, and the hosts The Hague Cricket Club. We are also due to meet the Dutch national team on Saturday as the showpiece finale to the tournament. Our first match was against The Flamingoes. They seemed a reasonable side, but it was clear by lunch when our batters had started to flay their attack around that we would not be very pushed to beat them. It was then that Les reappeared looking very shaken. He had been formally charged with attempting to enter the country with an illegal passport. He was interrogated by Dutch Immigration Officers for three hours, and they had confiscated his passport as evidence. He had been called a liar several times, and told that he could end up going to prison. He had seen another man who was being held for questioning sitting in a cell totally naked, and naturally was now in a bit of a state. They seemed to think that he had altered the date of birth entry in his passport by one year, from 1952 to 1953. Les strenuously denied it. He had travelled all over the world on that passport for nearly ten years.

Eventually they released him on a seven-day pass, but he is deeply worried. How will he get back into England with no passport? Will he end up on criminal files now he has been charged? And will he be found guilty at the end of it all? The British Ambassador is dealing with Les's case personally.

We beat the Flamingoes very easily, and the Hague Cricket Club too, but we ended up losing a very tight match against the MCC. There was no doubt that had we wanted we could have won it by running in and bowling properly. But it was a festival, and although none of us enjoyed losing, we would have looked ridiculous tearing in and bowling flat out on the matting. The Dutch team paid for that defeat the following day. We bowled with much more feeling to show that we could take our cricket seriously. There had also been a lot of loose talk through the bottom of beer glasses after the MCC game. The Dutch seriously fancied themselves to beat us. We showed them that there is an enormous gulf between them and us by bowling them out for 100, and knocking off the runs with twenty overs to spare. The cricket generally was great fun, and played in the right spirit. The only mishap was Laurie Potter breaking a finger.

I felt we were a little harsh on the Dutch. We should have batted first and put on an exhibition, to entertain the crowd. By bowling first, the match was over by three o'clock. However it was decided that we would bat for a further fifteen overs for the benefit of the late comers.

Peter Willey hardly had a great time. He refused to socialise and then had a nightmare against the MCC, which unfortunately for him contained a couple of ex-Northants players, Mushtaq and George Sharp. Will dropped a sitter off me at slip, and then the fellow he dropped slogged him for 35 off two overs. He in fact bowled three, but one was a maiden. We all fell about laughing as the ball peppered the tennis courts and sightscreen, and Will was fuming. He hates being hit about at the best of times, but in a joke match he just cannot take it all. He was busily threatening everyone, particularly me, and at the tea break, Mushtaq inscribed his bowling figures in enormous letters all over the mat in chalk:

P.WILLEY = 3 - 1 - 35 - 0

That finished Will off. He tore out of the pavilion in front of all the members and physically attacked Mushy. People rushed out to make sure that he did no serious damage to the little Pakistani, but it did illustrate another Willey humour failure. The umpire was not too amused either. As he put the bails on the stumps after tea, he glanced at the graffiti on a length and said: "You know, we cannot clean these wickets. That will still be there in four years time" Poor Will!

He also refused to come on a day trip to Amsterdam. The whole team went together in a couple of mini buses our hosts had laid on for us. But he stayed behind and watched the Test Match on TV. The lads were horrified. We were on social trip which had done so much for team spirit, and here was our senior pro refusing to join in because he would rather watch television.

Amsterdam was hilarious. We all piled on a boat for the obligatory tour round the canals. Then it was down to the red light district. There had been a documentry on the place on TV just before we left. But I was still amazed. Scantily-clad girls — at least most of them were female, I think — lounging about in shop windows, literally up for sale. They would flaunt themselves at us, pouting their lips, waiting to be approached. Of course after all the he-man talk on the bus, no-one even dared to tap on a window and chat to the girls. It is always the same.

Les had his own ideas: "It's like a bloody car boot sale in Shilton" he declared. We wandered those streets for a bit, feeling very self conscious.

Several times we were asked if we wanted drugs. Anything ranging from hash to heroin. I think most of us were relieved when five o'clock came, and we piled back on board the mini bus for home. Will was the main topic of conversation on the way back. We all know that underneath he has an excellent sense of fun, but he just seems to refuse to let it come out. Our dressing room revolves around friendly mickey-taking, with everyone giving as good as he gets. We all respect Will as a fine player, but wish he would relax a bit and join in. He seems so morose at the moment. I know that he is not happy with his form and that does affect him terribly. He gets himself into moods, and cannot snap out of them. Certainly a grumpy, out-of-form Will is to be avoided.

Naturally Les and I stayed together. We were looked after magnificently by an English family, Bill and Anna House, and their sons Jamie and William. They are cricket fanatics. All the lads did well with their hosts except Pottsy who had rough time. He was staying with Peter Such at the back of the ground with a lovely family and their four foot tall dog. It was an ugly, curly-haired hound which terrorised some of us in the nets, and it positively hated Pottsy. It attacked him one evening in the garden and sunk it's teeth deep into his leg. Poor Laurie had to have a tetanus injection from the local doctor which was administered in front of everyone in the bar! The real irony is that the dog loved Suchy, and the two regularly played ball together in the garden.

Les abroad is great value. He decided to take control during our excursions, but found that he was rather out of his depth when it came to speaking the local lingo. Our address was "Frankenslag", the "slag" being pronounced "shlarck". Les was having none of it, and one evening as we clambered into a Taxi, he demanded to be conveyed to "slagsville". That was a better effort than one of our senior players. After a couple of drinks one evening, he called a cab, got in and then could not remember where he lived. After trying every road in the district which ended in "weg", he spent a very long night in the marquee at the ground!

We had the Sunday off so Les and I took a stroll along The Hague's equivilent of the prom. We found that the Dutch are great starers and we both felt extremely uncomfortable after only a few minutes. We decided to split up to see if that made any difference. I did not think so, but Les claimed that no one stared at him at all. We decided that it was either my fairly loud sweater which was to blame, or they all thought we were a couple of homosexuals. Although I love my sweater I will hold that responsible! We stopped for lunch at a seaside cafe and when we received the menus we realised that we were in trouble. We could not understand a word. After half an hour of wondering what on earth we were going to do, once again Les took command.

"We'll order a couple of cheese omlettes,"he decided. "We can't go wrong then."

3-1-35-0: Will can't face it.

Graham Morris

The waitress turned up and we gave our order. "Excuse me," I said. "What is this?" pointing to a totally unpronouncable word. With a grin she took hold of Les's menu, and turned it to the back. There was a complete menu in English! Slightly embarrassed does not describe how we felt!

It was a weary party which made its way back to East Midlands Airport on Tuesday morning. Thankfully Les got through Immigration alright, but without his passport. That is still confiscated and he is still waiting to hear what will happen to him.

The hospitality had been marvellous, highlighted by the very posh dinner to celebrate the host club's centenary. The Dutch wore dinner jackets, and the "do" was held in one of The Hague's top hotels. One hundred and thirty men were packed into the plush ballroom, and our lads settled themselves in for a long boring evening. We had already been told that there would be seven official speeches. The Dutch promptly broke into a riot of filthy songs, bellowed at full volume. Things were thrown in the air, people danced on the tables, and the dinner was complete chaos. We held back for a bit, unsure if this was the normal course of events at a Dutch dinner. Apparantly it was, and it was not long before English accents could be picked out among the rugby songs. The Mexican Wave was particularly popular, and made several appearances.

The highlight of the evening was a speech by the President of the squash club, which is affiliated to the cricket section. As soon as the fellow stood up, he was treated to a series of Mexican Waves. Undeterred he soldiered on. Ten minutes passed, while we were informed about how the squash section was formed in 1932, and more Mexican Waves flashed around the room in an attempt to get the man to sit down. The MC told him to wind up. He ignored it all. There was now uproar in the room. Napkins were being hurled in the air, and boisterous songs made the speech inaudible. Still he carried on until the MC walked the length of the room, and amid loud cheers found a telephone and shouted at the top of his voice: "Oi! It's for you!"

That finished him competely, and reluctantly he sat down.

The cricket had not been very taxing, and we did not want it to be. The main thing was that we kept ourselves together and improved our team spirit during a lengthy lay off. We have three days to get ourselves back into the swing of things before meeting Surrey at The Oval on Saturday. I think we will need at least that long to recover from the hospitality.

CHAPTER FIVE

Close Encounters

9 June

I received a postcard at Grace Road this morning, postmarked Lima. It read:

Dear Jon,
On behalf of the cricket loving public here in Peru, I should like to say how sorry we are that you were overlooked by the England Selectors. It was a travesty of justice. Hoping you have better luck for the next Test. Andrew Symington

I was incredibly touched. I have had great public sympathy over the past week, even in Holland, but to think that someone thousands of miles away in Peru felt strongly enough to write means something. I wish Mr Symington had put his address on the bottom so I could thank him properly. It was then that I spotted a newspaper with the headlines about Mike Gatting's alleged night of passion with a local waitress in a Leicestershire hotel. Lies or not, the incident cost him his job.

I have always believed that cricket is a tough enough job when I take care of myself. Early nights after a hard day are my trademark. In being up late drinking with a barmaid during a Test Match, Mike clearly overstepped the mark. Thousands of cricket lovers paid a lot of money to watch him bat the following day. As public entertainers, it is our duty to provide the paying public with something for their money. That means we should be in the best physical shape possible.

Gatting could have let himself down the following day. He did only score a handful of runs before being bowled by Marshall and he could have let down the whole team too. His team. As captain, it was his responsibility to lead from the front. England were fighting to avoid an eleventh

79

consecutive defeat at the hands of the West Indies.

So another England captain bites the dust. Who should take over? I hope it is David Gower. He has learned a lot since he last had the job, and I know that he would love to have another crack. John Emburey is another candidate, but he had a disappointing First Test, and his place is not secure. He is not an experienced captain either, and he plays for Middlesex. I think it would be a little insensitive of even these England selectors to make Embers captain with Mike Gatting still his county skipper. Kim Barnett and Mark Nicholas are in with a shout but neither has played for England and, particularly in Nicholas's case, is not likely to. No, Gower is my man.

June 11

Britannic Assurance County Championship
Surrey 179 all out: Clinton 59; De Freitas 5 for 43; Agnew 1 for 63
Leicestershire 23 for 0

My car has been done again. I do not know why we keep staying at this hotel. The car park is right on a main road near the Oval. I suppose I should not be too surprised to find my window smashed. I was in a filthy mood by the time I got to the ground.

We view Surrey as one of the toughest matches of the season. Not because they have a terribly strong side, but because lurking in their team is one Sylvester Theophilus Clarke. Off the field he is a jolly nice bloke, apparently. I would not know. All I do know is that on the pitch he is a complete maniac. He bowls at a frightening pace, and he loves to have a go at the tailenders. You can keep your Marshalls, Pattersons and Daniels, this man is the most feared in county cricket and the Surrey lads know it. I got on to the ground quite early to have a look at the wicket. It was damp and fairly green. Clarke must be fit. I had a loosen up, and then got into the nets. Surrey's other overseas fast bowler, Tony Gray, was charging in, and it began to look as if he would be playing instead of Clarke. Under normal circumstances, Gray is a formidable enough opponent. Compared to Clarke, he is cannon fodder. After a couple of routine inquiries, which I am sure the Surrey lads get on the first day of every match "Cor. Tony looks fit. I guess he's playing today." Or "It's probably a bit cold for Sylvers today isn't it?" I quickly realised that Gray was injured.

Suddenly there was a kind of hush all over the ground. I turned around, and saw several of our lads looking in the direction of the pavilion. Coming down the steps was none other than him. Clarke.

Normally at this stage blind panic takes over. "I did bring that extra bit of padding down, didn't I?" "My life assurance is fully paid up." "Oh dear, I think I have just gone in the hamstring." But today was different.

THE MEAN MACHINE: Sylvester Clarke.

David Munden

Our man did not seem at all happy. He did not want to play. I dispatched George, who understands Clarke's Barbadian accent rather better than I, to listen in on the conversation between Clarke and Ian Greig, his captain. It seems that he has a sore knee which will not stand up to three days. Greig tried to make him change his mind, but to no avail. No Clarke and no Gray. The feeling is hard to describe. Almost like a stay of execution. I bumped into Clarke on the way back to the pavilion.

"Hullo Sylvers mate. How are you? Fit and raring to go?"

"No man. I've got a sore knee. I'm not playing today."

"Oh dear, let's hope it's nothing too serious. It would be a shame to really knacker it up."

Surrey are severely depleted through injury and illness. Their team reads like a second eleven. We stuck them in and bowled them out cheaply according to plan, but then bad light cut the day short by an hour. After a fortnight's lay off, bowling felt strange. I got through 27 overs by just after tea, and bowled my old mate Monte Lynch. But that ankle is bothering me again.

On the way down to see their physio, I bumped into Micky Stewart. He and I get on well, and I believe that he is on my side as far as England selection goes. He had a go about the pitches we have been bowling on, and even suggested that this one was a seamer's paradise. That was untrue, and I leapt down his throat . . . only to see him winding in a pretend fishing rod!

The physio took one look at my ankle and said: "You know what you've got don't you? Ballet dancer's ankle!" I warned him that if any of the lads got to hear about his diagnosis, I would personally strap him to his machines and turn them up full.

12 June

Refuge Assurance League

Leicestershire 158 for 8: Potter 41; Agnew 18 not out
Surrey 159 for 6: Agnew 1 for 34
Surrey won by 4 wickets

Another disastrous Sunday performance. We are now second from bottom of the Refuge Assurance League. The feeling afterwards in the dressing room was of deep depression. Daffy summed up exactly how we all felt.

"For Christ's sake lads, we're the best side in the country. Why can't we win a bloody one-day match?" The cold fact is that we cannot bat properly. Today we had a terrific start, 70 for one off 20 overs, then it all went wrong again. Gower played the kind of shot a batsman on the village green would have been embarrassed about, and the wheels fell off. Willey cannot get a run at the moment, and I found myself at the crease fending off the rabid Clarke with six overs left. He tore in, and ripped one into my gloves.

He is a shocker to face. He bowls very wide of the crease which means that the ball is angled into a right hander's body, and he bowls at the speed of light with a very quick action. People have questioned his action in the past, but he has been filmed by the TCCB, and was given the all clear. Apparently he has a very strange shoulder joint. I managed to slog him for four which made my day. It went like a bullet through mid on. Sylvers was not impressed, and gave me one of his stoney stares, but Daffy and I gritted our teeth and at least got a reasonable score. Ian Greig bounced me, which somehow I hooked for four. It was very satisfying because there is a bit of history between Greiggy and myself. It dates back to his time at Sussex, when in the middle of a particularly unpleasant, aggressive match he claimed that I threw the ball. I was outraged. It is the biggest insult that can be levelled at a bowler. I knew that my action was totally legitimate, but naturally I was concerned. Did everyone think that I was a chucker? Is there something in my action that makes it look suspect? For the next couple of years Ian and I had a real dingdong on the field, with me trying to tear his head off.

We never mixed off the field, until we came across each other in Sydney. We were both playing for clubs, and Chris Cowdrey, who was my captain there, decided that we had to bury the hatchet. Ian and I got talking, and have been the best of mates ever since. I did not play against his brother Tony, but Ian seems to be the same sort of character; absolutely committed on the field, incapable of giving less than 100 per cent. I now have enormous regard for him as a cricketer, and I have a sneaky suspicion that he thinks I am not too bad either. We still play it very hard against each other on the field, with both of us giving the other plenty of short stuff. But it is now out of mutual respect rather than hatred.

That is one of the great things about cricket. Once I would never have thought that I would ever be in a bar buying Ian Greig, the man who called me a chucker, a drink. But socialising afterwards is such an important part of the game.

I always enjoy going back to The Oval for two reasons. The first is because of the time I spent there as a youngster. I started out with Monte Lynch, Jack Richards and David Smith, and we have remained friends. The atmosphere there has completely changed since the mid Seventies. Then John Edrich was captain. I was terrified of the man. He believed that youngsters should be seen occasionally, and certainly never heard. It was all rather unpleasant. Now it is different, helped enormously by the presence of Geoff Arnold as county coach. He was one of the biggest characters in the game and has an awful lot to offer to Surrey's youngsters. It is a pity the set up was so harsh ten years ago.

The second reason is because it was at The Oval that I took the wickets of Viv Richards and Gordon Greenidge on the Saturday of my first Test. I will never forget either moment. Bev and my parents were there amongst the packed house, and I know that Dad got quite emotional. For him it was like a dream. He loves his cricket, and always went along to the Old Trafford Test when he was young. Never in his wildest dreams did he ever imagine that I would play for England.

13 June

Surrey 179 and 60 for 2
Leicestershire 255 for 7 dec.: Cobb 65; Briers 49; Agnew 18 not out

We did not get the big score we wanted, but things did not go our way. Gower was given out lbw for two when he had clearly hit the ball. David showed no emotion at all when the umpire's finger went up, he just tucked his bat under his arm and trudged off. It was a different story in the confines of the dressing room though. This is where people get David wrong. His critics thinks that he is very casual about the game, almost to the point of not caring. The truth is he cares deeply about both his and the team's performance. His reaction to getting out, especially if he has played an awful shot, turns the air blue. And players are uncomfortable when he gets out because they are not sure what to say to him. "Bad Luck" usually gets shouted down with "Bad luck? Rubbish!"

The thing that makes David different is that once he has settled himself down again, and cleared his mind, he will forget about it. As soon as half past six comes around, the last thing he will do is worry about cricket. I think that is a great attitude. There are several players in our side who could benefit from his example, players like Cobb and Whitaker, who worry terribly about their form. If they could learn to leave their cricketing thoughts behind at the ground with their kit every evening, it would make them more relaxed.

Philip Whitticase is another worrying about his batting. Two years ago when he first made the team, he showed a lot of potential as a number seven or eight batsman, but things have gone wrong since. He has struggled to get the ball off the square, which shows a lack of confidence. Today he even asked if he could bat below me, making me number eight. I agreed reluctantly, because the only way he is going to break his bad run is by batting and getting runs on the board. As it worked out he was in immediately after me anyway when Pottsy got out. He hit a couple of fours, and his impish grin returned. I think I might have a battle persuading him to bat number nine next innings!

Surrey were on level terms at the close. George and Daffy charged in and bowled with a lot of fire with the new ball. They got a wicket each, but then bowled a little loosely, which is easily done with very attacking fields. I am sure that Greiggy will be reluctant to leave us much of a target to chase, bearing in mind his weakened attack.

Met Robin Jackman afterwards in the Tavern. He pulled me aside as I was leaving for a parting word of advice. "Remember Spiro, make it impossible for them not to pick you. That was my theory, and it got me a couple of games. Good luck mate."

14 June

Surrey 179 and 291 for 8 dec.: Medlycott 71; Smith 59; De Freitas 4 for 114; Agnew 3 for 88
Leicestershire 255 for 7 dec and 38 for 2
Match drawn

One of the most disappointing day's cricket I have ever been involved in. If things had gone according to some sort of plan, we would have bowled Surrey out by mid-afternoon, leaving ourselves about 150 runs to win the match. But we made so many crucial blunders we wrecked our chance.

The first hour was a disaster. Gower opened with Daffy and myself, but bowled us from the wrong ends. There was a lovely warm breeze blowing across the ground from right to left, perfect for me to swing the ball away. It was humid and there was no doubt that the ball would go. Gower decided that Daffy, who bowls inswingers, should have that end. Peter Willey mentioned the wind direction to Gower as we got to the middle, but it made no difference. As a result, Daffy and I were trying to do each other's job. I ended up racing in trying to bowl flat out, and he struggled with the wind coming slightly into his face. It was a disaster. Medlycott took 13 off my first over, and then tucked into Daffy as well. The fielding was pathetic and we looked a shambles. Eventually Daffy trapped Monte Lynch lbw. Gower summoned us all together in the middle of the wicket, and blew a fuse. "Right you lot. This is an absolute disgrace. We look totally chaotic. We are supposed to be a side pushing for the Championship. If we carry on like this, we'll never win a match. It makes no difference who bowls where, let's just get on with it, and look like a decent outfit again."

The new batsman, David Smith, came out, and said: "Bloody hell Spiro, what's going off out here?" I shrugged my shoulders, and he said: "There have been some shots played haven't there? I couldn't watch, I had to go and hide with a newspaper!" They had noticed the shambles too. When the opposition can see it from their dressing room, you know things are bad. They were probably all having a great laugh.

Things got worse. I eventually got rid of Medlycott, which was an important wicket, and then got David Ward straight away. We felt the chance had come again now, but we had to get Smith out. In desperation I bounced him and he spliced the ball straight up in the air. It lobbed straight in between Daffy and Cobby on the leg side. They both started to go for it, and then at the last moment, both stopped dead. The ball fell right between them. There was a terrible silence before the hoots of derision from the crowd floated across the ground. It was diabolical. There was nothing anyone could say. I just glared. Daffy eventually got Smith caught behind and we were among the tail at 227 for eight, a lead of only 150. Immediately I bowled a short of a length ball at Feltham who edged it chest high to Gower's left at second slip. It did not go particularly fast, but the height was awkward. He dropped it. That was it. The tail enders did not give another chance. We had blown it. In the end they declared leaving us a ridiculous target of 216 in 28 overs. It was never on, but poor old Will sacrificed his wicket in the half-hearted attempt to score the runs at seven an over. The mood in the dressing room was glum. We are now seventh in the table. That is nowhere good enough and we know it. We should have won this match easily. We have no one to blame but ourselves.

15 June

Britannic Assurance County Championship
Leicestershire 313 for 7 dec: Potter 96; Whitaker 68; Agnew 5
Glamorgan 12 for 1

After the best part of a week away I found the lawns about two feet high, so tonight was put aside to getting the garden straight, and spending some time with Jennifer. She cannot understand why daddy has to go away from time to time. It is impossible trying to explain to a two and a half year old. I was talking to Nigel Briers about it the other day. He has a little boy a couple of years older than Jennifer. There are terrible scenes now when Nigel goes away. Young Michael cannot understand it, and begs Nigel to stay.

Once again we got the wicket wrong. It was supposed to be another green seamer, but did nothing. All around the country, sides are being skittled for 150 and less, yet it seems to be Grace Road which gets all the attention and accusations about pitch fixing. Our pitches of late have been about the mildest in the country and I wish they weren't.

Today was an absolute scorcher, and the forecast for tomorrow is the same. When I went out to bat, I remarked to umpire Jack Bond that the sun had caught his nose, and it looked like a red light outside a brothel.

"Bloody hell Aggers," he retorted in his high-pitched Lancastrian accent. "We could all get under yours and none of us would get slightly burnt!" Touche!

16 June

Leicestershire 313 for 7 and 14 for 0
Glamorgan 246 all out: Ferris 4 for 51; Agnew 3 for 94

I am sure I have said it several times before, but today was without doubt the best I have bowled in my life. I must have beaten the bat an average of three times an over for every one of the 36 overs I bowled. The batters could not lay anything on it, and when they did edge it, our slips dropped it. It was incredibly frustrating, because we could easily have taken twenty wickets today. My three for 94 looked ordinary on Teletext this evening. When I got home and gave Bev a kiss hello, she said: "You had a bad day. Didn't you bowl very well?" I had a chuckle. There are lies, damned lies and statistics.

I can hardly move now. There was no way anyone could get the ball out of my hand today, but I did not realise I had bowled so many overs. It is hard to know what made the ball do so much after doing absolutely nothing yesterday. The weather must have helped. It was cloudy and dull, with a high level of humidity. That normally helps the ball to swing, but today it was going off the seam. I held the ball exactly the same way for every delivery in those 36 overs, yet it moved a lot both ways. Normally I hold the ball with the seam pointing towards first slip, and the shiny side of the ball on the right hand side. That helps to make the ball swing away. If I want the ball to swing in, I simply reverse the shiny side of the ball, and open my chest out a bit in my delivery stride. It is important not to open out too much, because the batsman can spot it, and realise what you are up to. As far as seaming it is concerned, I leave that entirely up to luck. I know that 99 balls out of 100 hit the seam, and if that is happening, I will always have a chance of the ball doing something. That was the case today. I hit the seam every ball, and it moved. It did not matter that I did not know which way it was going to move. I simply held the same line of a couple of inches outside the off stump, and whichever way the ball moved, the batsman would have to play it.

It got to a stage where even the batsmen were asking what I had done to upset Him up there! Time and time again the ball flashed past the outside edge or ripped back over the stumps.

I felt that if I took one wicket early, I would run through them. Not only does it boost your confidence, but it makes the batsmen worry about you too. It is purely psychological, as most of the game is.

With Gower away Nigel Briers was in charge for the first time this year. He is a desperately keen cricketer, and Leicestershire born and bred. Leading the side means an awful lot to him. Today he did a good job, as he has many times before. He is the complete opposite to Gower, always encouraging the bowlers and motivating people on the field. Gower tends to believe that people should be able to motivate themselves, but Nigel always makes you believe that you are bowling well even if you know at times that you are not. I like his aggressive style. It rubs off on others.

Tomorrow morning we need another two hundred or so, and we should have a good game on our hands. Glamorgan have a record of playing boring cricket though. They usually seem content to get a draw out of game rather that going for a win. Last year they set us a ridiculous target of about eight an over for 30 overs and as soon as we hit one boundary, the fielders were scattered everywhere. At least by batting first we can set up the final day. I just hope that they go for the runs.

17 June

Leicestershire 313 for 7 and 164 all out: Agnew 12
Glamorgan 246 and 71 for 2: Agnew 0 for 16
Match drawn

I felt sorry for Nigel today. He desperately wanted the team to do well but was afraid to take any risk with the declaration. As a result he left it too late. The wicket was still misbehaving, and it was hard to score runs. I was sent in to try and have a bit of a slog with our lead standing at about 210 and 57 overs left. Nigel reckoned we wanted another 40 runs in eight or nine overs. The ball was literally flying off a length at times. I got one in the ribs from John Derrick, and then poor old Peter Hepworth, who was making his first class debut, got one which reared straight up on to his gloves and on to his wicket. Phil Whitticase got a similar one, and we were getting nowhere fast. George came out, and he called me for a discussion in the middle of the pitch.

"We've got to block out for a quarter of an hour." I thought he was joking. The ball was going everywhere, and the Glamorgan lads were not fancying the idea of facing us again. It was clear that they would simply try to survive and play out time.

"I'm serious man. We've got to make it safe." So George and I blocked it up, with the ball still seaming and bouncing awkwardly. Eventually he got out, and Les strode to the wicket.

"Here comes a man set on getting a hundred," joked Greg Thomas. With Les at the other end, there is only one thing to do. I played a few shots, and then holed out. I was not convinced that we had played it right. I can sympathise with Nigel, but I think that if he had been doing the job more often, and had more confidence in his own ability as a captain, he would have been more positive. As it was, we got a couple of them out, but we always knew that we would run out of time. The light was bad too, and we were going through the motions by the finish.

It was the first time that I have enjoyed playing against Glamorgan.

That may sound unkind, but they are now a side to be reckoned with on the field, and a super bunch of lads off it. When I first started, they were easily the weakest team in the Championship, and played some awful cricket. They were also a very anti-social lot. A new era has dawned in Wales. They have two very talented cricketers in Greg Thomas and Matthew Maynard, experience in Alan Butcher and Rodney Ontong, and a very approachable skipper in Hugh Morris. We meet again in Neath later in the season over four days, and I am looking forward to it.

We play Sussex tomorrow on a bright green wicket which I think will behave much as this one has. If it is sunny and we win the toss we should bat first. There is just one drawback. A certain Imran Khan has been persuaded to turn out for his beleaguered county tomorrow. I am surprised because there is a history of violence on the field during Leicestershire/Sussex matches, and Immy knows that he has got it coming to him, not least from me. He nearly killed me with a bouncer last year at Hove. I will never start a battle with a fast bowler, but once someone decides to have a go at me, I am happy to take up the challenge. Imran knows that I owe him one. I will have to ensure I get in first this time.

18 June

Britannic Assurance County Championship
Sussex 159 all out: Imran 55; De Freitas 5 for 38; Agnew 3 for 50
Leicestershire 102 for 4

We would have settled for that first thing this morning when we won the toss. The wicket was green again, but did not do very much. Sussex threw their wickets away, and Daffy's five wicket haul was a joke. He ran in like a ninety-year-old and bowled slower than Peter Such. He claimed that he had 'flu. If he was not fit, he should not have played. George and I just looked at each other as one by one he snared his victims. After all the playing and missing by the Glamorgan lads over the past few days, and then he turns up and makes a mockery of it all. One of the Sussex players, who will remain nameless, actually came up and apologised for getting out to Daffy! He was highly embarrassed. It will be interesting to see what the papers all say tomorrow. "Fiery De Freitas rips out Sussex" no doubt. George said that if that was the case, he would sue for libel! Anyway, our batsmen battled along, with Peter Willey scoring an unbeaten 52.

At the close of play Nigel called a team meeting. He said that he was a different type of captain to Gower and then reeled off a list of things he was not happy with. Any field changes the bowler wants to make have to go through him (fair enough), and if he does not agree with them, tough. (Not so fair enough. The bowler knows what he is trying to do, and nine times out of ten should have the field he wants). He then asked if there was anything that anyone else wanted to discuss.

I said I was sick of the batsmen moaning about the wickets, and blaming them for not being able to score runs. It was agreed at the beginning of the season that our best chance of winning the Championship would be by leaving more grass on the pitch to achieve more pace. It does not matter who scores runs as long as everyone chips in. It is supposed to be a team game. People are now thinking about their own performances too much.

There had also been too much talk recently of our seam attack not being good enough. That had mainly come from Willey, the batsman with most worries about his own form. He is happy to blame the wickets for that, but then accuses us of not winning matches on dodgy tracks. The answer to that is simple; the wickets have not been as difficult as people would like to think. I should know, I have bowled on them all. It is easy for an out-of-form batsman to blame the wickets for his poor performances, but the four fast bowlers are tired of accusations of incompetence. I have got 43 wickets. George, Daffy and Chris Lewis all 30 odd. If Paul Parker, the Sussex captain, knew that we were all sitting there having a go at our bowlers, he would kill himself laughing. That was when the discussion really got out of hand.

Ken Higgs, our coach, suddenly waded in. "I reckon I could have bowled them out for less than 100 on there." There was a silence while the bowlers looked at each other and then uproar.

I said: "I know that you were a great bowler Ken, but so too is Imran. He's got one wicket out there this afternoon. I think that what you've just said is ridiculous."

Nigel stepped in: "Look, this was not supposed to be a time to have a go at our bowlers. As far as I am concerned they have been magnificent."

I said: "That's fair enough Nige, but we're sick of what's being said by the others, and now by Higgy too. Either we continue our policy of having green wickets, or we forget the whole thing. But these wickets have not done as much as people would like to think they have."

Higgs had the last word. "Well, I can tell you that if there was more competition from the second team lads, you four would all be in there!" The meeting broke up then. No one took that last comment seriously. Higgy has the unfortunate habit of shouting his mouth off like that. It is better to ignore it totally than get involved in another argument. He only has the team's success at heart, and he is clearly getting frustrated by our poor results. The reasons for those have been a shortage of runs in limited overs cricket, and we have dropped vital catches in the three-day games. We all know that.

We are a team, and a bloody good one at that. If we stick together, and play hard every day, then we should get back up the table again. If we carry on like this, with more of these meetings, then we might as well forget it, and come back again next April. There are some volatile characters in our camp; Daffy, myself, Will, Whitaker, Nigel. We all like to have our say. We must get everyone working in the right direction and fast.

19 June

Refuge Assurance League

Sussex 182 for 4: Agnew 0 for 38
Leicestershire 179 for 7: Agnew 0 not out
                    Sussex won by 3 runs

When will we ever win a Sunday league match? I think we are now bottom of the league, and we deserve to be. Today we hit rock bottom by losing to Sussex, a match we looked like winning all the way until we lost quick wickets and hit the panic button. The only good thing to come out of the match was the excellent batting of two of our youngsters, Peter Hepworth and Justin Benson. They came together at 98 for five, and came so close to knocking off the runs. Imran's bowling did not bother them at all, in fact they treated him with complete contempt. But with three runs wanted off the last three balls, disaster struck. Benson smashed a Pigott delivery straight back. It looked a certain four from the moment it left his bat, but it struck Heppers straight in the midriff. The ball bounced out to extra cover, Hepworth staggered out of his ground to attempt a suicidal single, and was run out by the swooping Parker.

I was next in. But Rambo missed the next ball and was bowled. Then George failed to make contact with a perfect yorker last ball and we lost the game. People ask what it is like batting at times like that. They imagine we must be nervous. But the answer is that it is much easier to go in then rather than, say, three overs before the end. There is no real pressure. I could either have got out going for the winning runs, in which case people would say "well, at least he tried", or I could be a hero. The bowler feels exactly the same at that stage. I had a laugh with Lester Piggot. The poor fellow, went through the same thing last week too. Today he was the hero, and was mobbed by the Sussex fans as he left the field. Another day, in the identical situation, we would win. It is for this reason — that Sunday cricket is such a lottery — that the majority of players hate it. I suppose it is for the same reason that the public love it. For me the only thing good about Sunday cricket is for the blooding of youngsters. Today our two lads were great. They raced about like greyhounds in the field, and then showed that they could cope with pressure as well.

While they felt terrific, I felt bloody awful. It has been a hell of a few days. It started with those 36 overs on Thursday. Then it was twelve more on Friday, fifteen yesterday, and the statutory eight today. No wonder I feel knackered. I love bowling, and would much rather be in action than standing about in the field, but this is where county cricket lets itself down.

I bowled a lot at the Oval, too, and it is all beginning to take its toll. My left ankle is having to be heavily strapped now to get me through the day. Even so, it is very difficult to come back and bowl after my first spell because of the pain. It is on my mind now. I know that it is going to be very sore when I bang my ankle into the ground as I bowl. As a result, my brain makes me pull back, and I do not bowl as quickly as I should. It will need a rest at some stage. The West Indies match next month would seem ideal. The trouble is, everyone will be trying to miss that one. There is too much cricket without a break. It leads to players getting injured and disillusioned with the game. We would perform better if we played less, because we would be fresher, both physically and mentally. I know that I am tired at the moment, and it is starting to show. Apart from the pain from my ankle, my bowling was inconsistent today. I could not get fully loose, and my whole body ached. I hope that a system of 16 four-day matches is introduced soon. It will mean less cricket, but the standard will improve. As for now, I can see little respite. We are batting in our current game. But we have already lost four wickets, so we will have a good bowl again tomorrow and Tuesday. Then we have got the first round of the Nat-West on Wednesday.

Did not get the chance to chat with Imran about the three-day wicket, but I will tomorrow. I am sure that he will laugh at the suggestion that we should have got them all out for 100. He is one of the greatest fast bowlers the game has ever seen. He has also bowled on this wicket. I would rather take his word for it.

The feeling in the dressing room was still tense today. There are definitely two factions — batsman and bowlers.

20 June

Sussex 159 and 101 for 3
Leicestershire 309 all out: Willey 130; Hepworth 51; Agnew 22; Pigott 6 for 100

Thank goodness Willey has got some runs at last. That should ease the pressure. He played really well too, despite being hit in the face by a beast of a ball from Imran. It hit his shoulder before cannoning into his jaw, but the force still knocked a back tooth out. Will just spat it out in typical fashion, and got on with batting. Peter Hepworth again showed a lot of maturity during his 51. He is the most unlikely looking sportsman, tall and gangly, with a scholarly face emphasised by a large pair of spectacles. He would look more at home in a cassock singing hymns in Canterbury Cathedral, but he has shown us all that he can bat. He is technically very correct, like his coach and mentor, one Geoff Boycott. It was Boycott who told him to sign for Leicestershire rather than Yorkshire. Peter's dad and Sir Geoff were good mates, and played club cricket together. Although he

FOUR MORE: Willey in form at last.

David Munden

played extremely well today, he found a few problems dealing with Imran. He met up with Willey in the middle of the pitch, and their conversation went something like this:

"Excuse me Will, I'm struggling a little bit with Imran. How do you try and play him?"

"From the other bloody end!" came the reply. Heppers pushed his glasses back on his nose, and set off back again none the wiser!

I got in to bat just as the second new ball was being taken. It always seems to happen. I walk out just as the fast bowlers are warming up, armed with the new missile, and hell bent on improving their bowling figures by ripping through the tail. Phil Whitticase always finds himself in the same position. And here we were again, fending off Imran, and a particularly hostile Lester Pigott. Eventually I started to attack anything bowled in my direction. Imran was clearly tired, but at the end of an over he shouted to Paul Parker: "I'll have one more if he's facing," (with the emphasis very much on the he, accompanied by an icy stare in my direction at the non strikers's end). Now Philip and I had a problem. We were both playing positively, hitting the bad ball for four and having a real go at the good ones too sometimes. But we had to make sure that he was facing for the start of Imran's next over. Paul Parker was running down the wicket towards me after having a word with Lester and I stopped him as he got level. "Skipper, can we just clarify one small point here? Who is it who has to be at which end in order for him not to bowl any more?"

"Aggers old boy. If I were you I would play six of the best forward defensive strokes you have ever played to the next six balls, and make sure you stay down here. That way you should be OK."

I thanked him for his concern, and indeed managed to block the first two balls. Then I had a nightmare. I edged the third down towards third man. There was only a single there, and we took it. I was now at the wrong end. Jack Bond confirmed that there were three balls left. I glanced down to fine leg where the man himself was limbering up, looking particularly mean. Whitticase shouldered arms to the next two deliveries. There was one to go. I was desperately trying to catch his eye. Eventually he looked up.

"For God's sake Roddy, get a single you little swine. Just get a bit of bat on it, and I'll be down there." Roddy the Rat — so called because, like all wicket-keepers, his kit stinks — looked down and grinned.

"Rat, it's in your interests too. Get down here, and he's off!" Desperation was setting in now, but good old Phil hit the last ball into the covers, and we completed an easy single. That was accompanied by some foul sounding Pakistani oath from the boundary, and I was saved.

We took to the field with a handy lead of 150, and immediately George got a wicket.

I got Parker lbw, and then the mighty Khan himself, caught behind off a beauty which swung away late.

I WANT HIM: Imran signals his intentions.   David Munden

We took tea very pleased with ourselves, but now Sussex dug in, and we did not bowl as well as our pre-tea spell. George had some problems no-balling, and so as a remedy I asked Jack Bond, the umpire, to stand back another foot or so. That often brings a bowler back by the same distance, and so stops him overstepping the front line. I explained the theory to Bondy who was happy to oblige.

"Anything to stop him bloody no-balling," he said. I should have known. The very next ball Bondy shouted "No ball" and looked straight at me.

"Bloody hell, Aggers. He was nearly at Toddington services when he let that go. Bugger that. I'll stand where I was!" Another theory bites the dust!

21 June

Sussex 159 and 210: Pigott 56; Agnew 4 for 70
Leicestershire 309 and 61 for 2
Leicestershire won by 8 wickets

Our first win for six weeks, but we made hard work of it. The morning session was just like The Oval, with people shouting at each other and tempers frayed. It all stemmed from Daffy's apparant lack of effort. He is still suffering from a cold, and says that it affects his breathing. His bowling was again barely medium pace, and the rest of the team was furious. Then he walked off the field, saying he needed some medicine. That meant that we were down to ten men on the field. The aggression we had built up and were channelling at the batsmen disappeared and we looked lost. Lester was slogging the ball around, helped by the fact that we were a man light, and for some time we looked dreadful. Eventually Daffy reappeared at the gate, and I signalled for him to come back on as I was bowling at the time. He walked up to me smiling all over his face. I turned on him. "I don't know what the bloody hell you're laughing at mate. That was a disgrace." He ignored me totally.

Gower is back tomorrow. After today's Test defeat I am sure the last thing he feels like will be a Henry Kissinger job with Daffy again. It will be interesting to see if Daffy plays tomorrow. He has a problem. He has to show the lads that he was really poorly to have to leave the field today, and the easiest way of doing that is to rule himself unfit. Gower will say that surely he can play with a cold, and then we are back to square one again.

"We've decided to change our name from Sussex to Macintosh, because we're always getting pissed on!" They were Alan Wells' parting words this afternoon. They are not the strongest side in the Championship, but they are certainly one of the friendliest. It has been a fun four days. They were not helped by a final scorecard which had two retired hurts and an absent injured on it. Alan Wells was hit on the forearm by George in the first innings and could not bat second time around. Exactly the same thing happened to Alan Green last night from Daffy's loosener, and then I broke Neil Lenham's finger this morning. That meant that we only had to take seven wickets in their second innings for them to be all out. Bad luck for a side who are struggling anyway.

We have to dispose of Suffolk in the Nat-West tomorrow. There is nearly always one major shock at this stage of the competition. Suffolk have a few useful players, including Chris Gladwin, who played a lot of games for Essex. They will not be a pushover.

22 June

Nat-West Trophy

Leicestershire 255 for 9: Gower 99; Agnew 1
Suffolk 168 for 6: Agnew 0 for 25
Leicestershire won by 87 runs

At least we did not fall foul of a minor county. Northants did. Cheshire beat them by one wicket. It must feel humiliating. Our game was tedious. The wicket was extremely slow, making stroke play difficult, and we would have to have bowled really badly to have lost.

We still looked too lethargic in the field. The trouble is that everyone is knackered. I counted up the overs I have bowled since the Glamorgan game, one week ago today. 96 I make it. Last year I bowled just under 800 in the season, and that was easily more than any other fast bowler in the country. That averages out at something like 45 overs a week.

I did not feel too bad until it came to bowling the first ball up the slope. I could not get there at all. In the end I bowled off a short run, and only got through seven of my allotted twelve overs. I think Gower saw that I was struggling and took pity on me.

We had a discussion after the match, and Gower has given us two days off. We are all aware that we have not really looked like our true selves the last couple of days. This break should recharge the batteries.

'I'M OVER HERE': The Rat finds the ground for once.

David Munden

CHAPTER SIX

Triple Gloucester

24 June

I went to the ground for treatment on my ankle this morning and met Mike Turner. He is concerned about the way we have looked on the field lately. Apparently the members have been giving him an ear-bashing. Turner is worried that we have lost the feeling of cohesion that we had six weeks ago at the start of the season.

I feel much fresher after two days off, but it was a terrible wrench saying goodbye this evening. Bev was very upset. This pregnancy is really getting her down, and Jennifer does not help much either. While I am away she runs Bev ragged. It is not pleasant to go away for four days leaving your wife in tears. There is also the problem of the second baby. It was confirmed today that it is due while we are in Chelmsford in September for the last match of the season. We will have to cross that bridge when it comes.

I brought The Rat down to Gloucester. He is the most incompetent navigator I have ever had the misfortune to travel with. We got completely lost trying to find the hotel. Once, after he had said confidently "Turn left here, and it should be on the right" we found ourselves in Safeways car park. Then we got trapped in a new housing estate. My name is on the side of the car as part of a sponsorship deal with a local garage, and I could see all the net curtains being pulled to one side. The locals must have wondered what on earth "Jon Agnew ... Leicestershire CCC and England" was doing turning round in their driveway. When we came to a grinding halt at the entrance of a Barratt Showhouse I stopped the car, hit Phil, and then we set about studying the instructions. Eventually we found the hotel. We were the last to arrive. Even Daffy had got there, on his own as well. The Rat felt suitably humbled.

25 June

Britannic Assurance County Championship
Leicestershire 189 all out: Briers 53; Agnew 11; Curran 4 for 55
Gloucestershire 92 for 6

A totally forgettable day. First I ran out poor Whitticase by most of the pitch, then I got "sawn off" lbw. Finally I failed to take a wicket. It was the first time I have ever run anyone out, and I felt dreadful afterwards. I pushed a ball from Curran to mid on and immediately shouted "Yes." However I had hit the ball much harder than I thought, and it went like a rocket straight to Bainbridge. I did not even move, but watched helplessly as Rat belted down the pitch towards me. I gulped a muffled "No. Sorry Rat," and he tried to get back. What made it worse was that he fell over as well, so he had no chance. He set off for the pavilion with a withering glare in my direction, muttering something about ten quid. We have a bet for that amount on the number of runs we score this season. He said later he reckoned I ran him out because he was catching up!

Umpire Barry Dudleston, the ex-Leicestershire batsman, and a very good friend said: "Look on the bright side, Aggers. You're on your way to taking a five. You've got one wicket already!"

George and I knuckled down and scored a few. The pitch was very, very slow, but moved off the seam, so scoring runs was very difficult. It was a grafting wicket. Terry Alderman, the Australian seam bowler, came on, and beat me all ends up with a jaffa which moved away late. At the end of the over I said: "Sorry Terry. That was far too good for me. You want to save them for someone who can bat a bit."

"Yeah mate. Tell you what Aggy, I couldn't get a root in a woodpile today!"

I laughed, without understanding the Aussie slang, and a few minutes later was trudging back to the shed, lbw Alderman. I swear that I had got a long way forward, but umpire Shepherd felt differently, and up went the finger. It was only the second time I have ever been lbw.

I had a chat with Shep, who is one of the nicest blokes on the circuit, and suggested that he was thirsty as it was tea-time! I told him to be ready as I was bowling from his end, and I expected some action after that decision.

I got nothing. I beat the bat heaps of times, but did not strike once. I could not even test Shep because I did not hit the pads either. Meanwhile at the other end, they were falling like ninepins. George got three quickly, and then Daffy struck twice, and we were in a commanding position. It is a vital game for both sides. They are only a handful of points above us. If we can get a good lead, we should win.

On the way back, Rat got us lost again. This time we ended up in a Wimpey Showhome. It is getting very embarrassing. He was happy to see

HUNGRY LOOK: David Shepherd strides off for tea.   David Munden

me distressed though. "Do you really need a tenner that badly, Aggers?"

26 June

Refuge Assurance League
Gloucestershire 202 for 9: Romaines 67; Agnew 2 for 24
Leicestershire 139 all out: Briers 54; Agnew 4
Gloucestershire won by 53 runs

Another shambles. When will we learn how to play Sunday cricket? It does not matter so much that we are losing; we all accept that Sunday cricket is a lottery, and the winning side is not neccessarily the best cricket team. It is how badly we are losing that is causing concern. We were never in the game today, and the whole performance was embarrassingly poor.

Barry Dudleston was just as disappointed. He questioned whether our batters really knew how to pace themselves in a one-day match. We are bottom of the league, and in that situation people really do not want to play on Sundays, me included. But we must do the job properly for professional pride.

Gower called a team meeting in our hotel this evening. We all assumed that it was to be an inquest into our Sunday performances, but it turned out to be a general discussion about how to get things back on the right track. He said: "Let's face it lads, we are out of the Benson and Hedges Cup, we are out of the Sunday league, and we are about sixth in the Championship. Hardly wonderful stuff. We have to get back to the hard grind of doing things properly. I am not going to set strict times for when you must do fielding practice and so on because that's not my style. We are professional cricketers, and must act responsibly."

We have let things like catching practice slip over the past few weeks. Critics who knew that could point to things today and say that it showed.

The trouble really started when Will suddenly accused Daffy of not trying against Sussex on that last morning. I closed my eyes waiting for the inevitable reaction, and sure enough Daffy exploded. He ranted and raved using foul language. But basically he accepted that he should not have left the field on Tuesday. Instead of leaving it there, Will carried on. He said that as long as things suit Daffy, he is alright. But if he cannot have the field he wants, or bowl from the end he wants, he does not try.

That was too much for Daffy. He walked out of the room hurling abuse at everyone. It is difficult to say what I thought at that moment. Will had said what everyone had wanted to say, but did not have the guts to. But having got the admission from Daffy that he had not done the right thing, he should have left it there. Daffy felt that he was being picked on, and reacted accordingly. The last thing that we wanted from that get-together

HITTING OUT: Daffy ... on the field and off.

David Munden

ACTION NOT WORDS: Daffy and Will didn't speak.　　David Munden

was a bust up. Yet that is exactly what we got. Nigel went to Daffy's room and calmed him down, and they both came back together. George then acted as mediator, saying that Daffy should learn to accept criticism, and the atmosphere gradually got better. The meeting broke up with everyone glad to get out. Daffy overreacted, but anyone who knows him would have guessed that he would walk out. He felt trapped, and unable to argue reasonably. I agree with most of what Will said, but the timing was unfortunate. This evening's meeting was to pick people up after a hard few weeks rather than an inquest. It seemed, too, that Gower was happy for Will to have his say, because at no point in the clash did he attempt to intervene. Only when Daffy stood up to walk out did Gower try and calm things down.

With the differences of opinions aired, most of us sat down together for dinner. I sat next to Daffy and said: "Your problem is that you are the team's barometer. When you are up, the whole team is firing because you have the ability to lift the whole side when you are steaming in. Take that Lancashire game in the Benson's. You were magnificent, and the whole team was on a high.

"Conversely, on that last day against Sussex you were down, and you dragged the team down with you. I know that it is an enormous responsibility for you to shoulder, but that is the effect you have on the team's performances." He listened. When he is firing on all cylinders he makes the team tick. We need him to do that as often as possible. I hope that this evening's discussion has not soured him again.

27 June

Leicestershire 189 and 162 for 7: Briers 51
Gloucestershire 142 all out: De Freitas 5 for 41; Agnew 0 for 15

I was the first down at breakfast this morning after an awful night in a bed at least a foot too short for me. Gradually the others followed, including Daffy. He seemed cheerful, and made no mention at all of the meeting. No one else said a word about it either. Later he ran in and bowled well. He is not talking to Will, and I can see that situation dragging on for ages, because both are too stubborn to take the first step towards reconciliation. They will both stay out of each other's way for a while, and that may well prove the best thing. The team can absorb one fall out like that without too much problem. It is when other people take sides that the trouble begins. I do not think that will happen. In our heart of hearts everyone in the team knows that what Willey said last night was what we were all feeling, including Daffy. I think he will now swallow his pride and get on with being the match-winner we all want him to be.

This match is beautifully poised. We need another 30 or so in the morning to set Gloucester a stiff total to chase on a wicket which is still doing it for the seamers. Nigel and Cobby played really well this afternoon, helped by a bit of good fortune. Then we collapsed dramatically, losing those two, Gower, Willey, Whitaker and Daffy in no time. Even if their batsmen get off to a good start tomorrow, we must keep going. It will be a tense afternoon.

28 June

Leicestershire 189 and 177: Briers 51; Agnew 4 not out; Curran 7 for 54
Gloucestershire 142 and 144: Agnew 6 for 39
Leicestershire won by 80 runs

Our second consecutive win, which lifts us to third in the table. It was also a timely haul of wickets for me. I was pleased with the way I bowled. The wicket still offered some help, but I put the ball in the right place at a reasonable pace. It has been some time since my last decent return, and this one took me past 50 wickets for the season. I am now just three short of 500 in my career.

Politics are still affecting relationships on the pitch. Whenever Daffy took a wicket today Will and Laurie Potter got in a huddle together and ignored him. There was also an incident this afternoon when Potter took a fine slip catch off me. Daffy came up and said "well done" to me but ignored Pottsy altogether. We are a team for God's sake. I can accept that there will always be differences of opinion off the field, and even people disliking others, but that must remain off the field. When we walk out on to the park, we are Leicestershire County Cricket Club; a unit, and we must play as a unit. People watching can quickly see if things are not right. Today it stuck out like a sore thumb. Gower or Nigel must get it sorted out or it will drift on and on.

I spoke to one of my favourite former cricketers, Tom Graveney. I have always found him approachable and helpful. I was interviewing him for *The Cricketer*. They want me to write about the security, or lack of it, in professional cricket, and I wondered what it was like in Tom's day. It was very enlightening. He started on £4 a week, and could not afford to buy a car until he had played for England for four years. Something he believed had changed over the years was the amount the players enjoyed playing the game. He reckons that today's players do not seem to get nearly as much fun out of it as he did. I am sure he is right. The pressure to win now is sometimes overpowering, and it does make the players wander around with the world on their shoulders.

I drove back along the M5 with Phil Whitticase this afternoon. We were listening to Wimbledon on the car radio when the sports desk came on.

"There are now real problems for the England cricket selectors."

106

(radio's volume is turned up a couple of notches).

"Paul Jarvis is rated extremely doubtful for Thursday's Test after breaking down this afternoon, and Nick Cook has a problem with his ankle. The selectors will make an announcement about strengthening the squad in the next hour."

"Bloody hell Aggy, they've got to pick you this time," said Phil. I was nervous, alright. I had just taken my fiftieth wicket of the season, and was bowling well. When Dilley was doubtful at Trent Bridge, they put Greg Thomas on standby. That was ridiculed by the Press, and the only bit of logic there was that Thomas is an out and out fast bowler, like Dilley. This time it is different. The next hour passed very slowly. My mind was racing.

At a quarter to six the sports desk came on again. "The England cricket selectors have announced that Glamorgan's Greg Thomas will be added to the squad for Thursday's Test at Old Trafford ... "

"Well, bugger me!" said Phil. That summed it up well. I thumped the steering wheel in sheer frustration. What more can I possibly do?

I will not let it get me down though. I will show them. One hundred wickets is my target again for this year. Then we will see what excuse they come up with for not taking me on tour.

1 July

A couple of days off certainly works wonders! I was excited as I drove up the M1 with Whitticase this evening. There is always something special about playing Yorkshire, especially at Headingley. I think it is their reputation for giving nothing away. Unfortunately, though, we made our way north through a deluge, and we could well be struggling to get much play in tomorrow.

My ankle is still sore, despite three days' treatment. It needs a lay off of at least a week, but I cannot afford that.

Les has made the trip up here, and we are reunited as roomies after several weeks apart. He has been struggling to regain his top form in the second team and was clearly depressed.

"I'll tell you what Aggy," he said. "It doesn't take long before they drag you down to their level." I sympathised with him. I knew what he meant. He has had the task of captaining the youngsters. A thankless task, but it does at least delay the inevitable boredom which quickly sets in after a couple of second class matches out in the sticks. Our second team this year is unusually weak and inexperienced, and poor old Les has found it hard work to keep himself going while trying at the same time to teach his students the basics of professional cricket. At least he is back in the first team again now. Daffy and Gower are away at the Test. Yorkshire have been having a rotten season, and have a stack of injuries. We need to win this one.

OOH, IT HURTS: Dickie Bird explains all.

David Munden

2 July

Britannic Assurance County Championship
Leicestershire 155 for 4 Willey 91 not out
v Yorkshire

A slow day on a wicket to match. The Headingley groundsman is obviously taking no chances with the Fourth Test only a couple of weeks away. This pitch is brown and flat, with no pace at all. We were put in to bat, and ground our way through most of the day until rain saved the spectators, and ourselves, from further punishment.

Dickie Bird is on duty again for these four days. I always enjoy his company, and called out to him from the dressing room as I saw him go by. "Morning Harold."

"Oh Jonathan," he replied with an agonised look on his face. "Please don't shout. I've got a huge boil the size of a cricket ball on my arse!"

Geoff Boycott called in to see us this afternoon. I always had the highest respect for him, and enjoyed bowling at him. It was always the ultimate challenge trying to dismiss the great Sir Geoffrey. I remember doing just that at a packed Headingley in a Bensons and Hedges match. Most of the crowd had turned up hoping to see their hero get some runs, but I got him cheaply. There was complete silence as he walked off that field. I think he enjoyed our tussles as well.

"Hello Aggers mate. Taking a stack of wickets again I see."

"Yes Fiery. I think all the batsmen these days must be blind!"

"Aye! You're right. And they're all playing at Old Trafford!"

Geoff was not impressed by England's performance against the West Indies, particularly in that Third Test. He claimed every batsman got himself out in the first innings. Not one was a genuine wicket. He questioned how much they wanted to play for England. How much it really meant to them? How much work they did to improve their game when they played a bad shot? He said that if he got himself out he was inconsolable for hours afterwards. It was the ultimate crime to throw your wicket away. Our batters listened to Geoff totally enthralled. Say what you like about the bloke, he was the model professional.

With the rain came the usual horseplay in the dressing room. My kit kept disappearing as I was packing it up. We have to travel to Hull tomorrow so all our stuff has to go too. The Raper was concealed in the toilet, my whites were hidden away under the seats, and my helmet had disappeared. I suspected The Rat, who was finding the whole thing very amusing. Then he made a fatal mistake. He left his best black shoes beside my chair and made a grab for them. I got them first, and lobbed them straight out of a frosted window into what I assumed was the car park. The Rat was far from happy, and was furious when he came back after an attempt to find them. They were stuck on a flat roof outside the window. It was also still pouring with rain. I told him to get a ladder.

So there he was with the attendant's step ladder in the pouring rain scrambling about on this flat roof with a large proportion of the crowd watching. I do not think he will mess with my kit again.

3 July

Refuge Assurance League

Leicestershire 172 for 4: Potter 66
Yorkshire 173 for 4: Sharp 56; Agnew 1 for 21
Yorkshire won by 6 wickets

Our seventh consecutive Sunday defeat, with the usual problems. At least for the first time this season we had wickets in hand for the last eight overs, but we did not use them.

Hull is not the most memorable of grounds. Many rely on a ring of mature trees to give them appeal. Hull is surrounded by railway tracks instead, and busy ones at that. Train after train rattled past. Part of the ground is used as a rugby pitch which meant that fielding on that area was a lottery. Poor old Heppers was posted down there, but he coped manfully. It is his home club ground, so he has something of an advantage.

There was an extraordinary scene after the match. Someone had pinched Nigel Briers' jockstrap and underpants. He had laid them out to dry outside our dressing room door after his innings and forgot about them while we fielded. Later he discovered that they had vanished. He drew the line at having an appeal made over the tannoy however, and finally conceded that one of the many autograph hunters must have nicked them to keep as some sort of trophy! Who on earth would be tempted to make off with one of Nigel's jockers I do not know.

The latest medical bulletin on Dickie's boil is that he spent a comfortable night after having a long soak in the bath in our dressing room at Headingley last evening. He is still far from happy though, and is considering having it lanced by the physio tomorrow.

4 July

No play. Rain

It took only a couple of tentative steps onto the Headingley outfield for Dickie Bird and Peter Eele to decide that there would be no play today. The whole ground was a foot underwater, and constant rain since has made prospects tomorrow bleak as well. At least today's abandonement came early. There is nothing worse than hanging round the dressing room all day just in case we might get an hour of play later. I went into Dickie's room to thank him for his prompt action, and asked him how his ailment was.

"It's like a flippin' turnip, Jonathan," he moaned. "A flippin' turnip."

We talked about the England team. Dickie feels strongly that umpires should have a say in selection, as they have the best view of everything that goes on. They can assess how well people are playing, but it seems that they rarely get consulted. Dickie believes that changes should be made, particularly among the batters. He is standing in the Test at Headingley, and whenever we talked about that match, he twitched. Surprisingly, he suffers badly from nerves.

5 July

Leicestershire 253 all out: Agnew 0. 2nd innings forfeited
Yorkshire 1st innings forfeited and 256 for 6: Love 68; Blakey 51; Agnew 0 for 78
Yorkshire won by 4 wickets

Our gamble failed. After all the rain, the only hope of a result was for us to forfeit our second innings, and for the Yorkies to chase our score. We felt that we had a good chance of bowling them out, not least because it was a gettable target, and so their batsmen would play their shots. They did, and they won. We took the risk because Yorkshire pose no real threat to us in the championship. They were third from the bottom, whereas we desperately needed a victory. Kent looked on course to beat Sussex, and that would really stretch their lead at the top. We would reckon to win half the matches played like this, and those odds were certainly good enough for us to have a go.

As it was, we were always one wicket behind. Jim Love played superbly. He put me into the back row of one stand for an enormous six. Will said it very nearly brought down the plane passing overhead at the time. He won them the match, and we have no complaints.

I had a very forgettable game. I was sent out to bat with the instruction to hit 14 runs off 5 balls to secure the third batting point. Phil Carrick was bowling and was well aware of the plan.

"It's you or me, Fergie," I shouted down the wicket. It was me. I had an enormous heave at the first ball and was clean bowled. My good pal Kevin Sharp escorted me off with his arm around my shoulder killing himself laughing. I told him that he was laughing too soon. It was his turn to bat next, and I have a good record against him.

Unfortunately he did me again. As he walked out to bat I felt him press a sheet of paper into my hand. I examined it. It was an application form to join the Primary Club — exclusively for those who have been out first ball.

On the day that England got thrashed in the Old Trafford Test, Brian

Close turned up to see us. Brian is renowned for his bravery and expertise when he faced quick bowling, and he was disgusted as together we watched the sorry procession of England's batsmen on TV. He was critical of their technique. He reckons that when facing fast bowlers you should get right back on your stumps, and then you are still in a position to get forward if the ball is pitched up. He believes too many players today try and play it off the front foot, and get stuck. He also made a comment which interested me. "The only difference between Test cricket and this (county cricket), is in your head. Either you can handle it or you can't. Too many of our players can't."

Several heads will probably roll after this debacle. I hope that Gower's will not be one of them. He has now played in 99 Tests. It would be cruel if he was to miss out getting to that magical 100. As for us, it's back down the M1. Gloucestershire face us tomorrow in the Nat-West, and it will not be easy.

6 July

Nat-West Trophy
Gloucestershire 273 for 5 60 overs: Bainbridge 89; Athey 62; Agnew 1 for 37
Leicestershire 46 for 1 20 overs
Match to resume tomorrow

We have let them get too many. About 240 was right on that wicket. Kevin Curran and Bainbridge went berserk at the end, flaying the bowling to all parts. Now the game looks beyond us. Cobby was needlessly run out this evening just to make matters worse.

One of my all time favourite men turned up today. Anderson Montgomery Everton Roberts, or Fruits to his mates, came back for the first time since leaving Leicestershire four years ago. On the field he was one of the finest fast bowlers the game has ever seen. Off it he is a thoroughly soft and rather shy fellow. He and I took the new ball together when he was with us. He taught me virtually everything I know about bowling and we became very close friends. Apart from putting on a few extra pounds here and there, he had not changed. When we broke off play because of rain, he immediately set up the table for a game of cards. There we were, reunited. Roberts, Agnew, Willey and Taylor playing Sweaty Betty. He plays cards exactly the same way as he bowled; displaying no emotion. But when he managed to do me a couple of times his whole frame rocked with silent laughter, and his round face lit up. The card would hit the table with a resounding thump, delivered with all his might. We have arranged to have a net together next Tuesday, before we travel to Old Trafford. He wants to bowl at me. I have told him he will need a whole bag of balls. I do not think I should have said that!

112

FRUITS IS BACK: The great Andy Roberts.

David Munden

TOUGH BREAK: The 'culprit', Phil Bainbridge.

David Munden

Gary Lineker also showed his face this afternoon. He was supposed to have played with our second team this summer after the European Soccer Championships, but was then struck down with hepatitis. He looked dreadful today, he must have lost a stone in weight. I hope he will be fit enough to start the new soccer season. Shame about the cricket as he is a more than useful batsman. I am sure that if he played, the second team would have more spectators than the first!

My day ended with disaster. I attempted a slower ball at Phil Bainbridge, who hit it like a bullet straight back. I did not see it until it was about a foot from my face. Desperately I stuck out my right hand. The ball hit it and dropped dead. I was convinced my hand was broken. Shooting pains went up my arm. I still had three overs to bowl. Somehow I got through them. Craig brought me an ice pack on the boundary, which numbed the pain for a while, but afterwards I was in agony. My hand is now like a balloon, swathed in bandages, and I cannot think I will be able to hold a bat tomorrow. Let us hope I am not needed.

A footnote to all that. At tea-time I was talking to Andy Roberts on the balcony. He asked me what different deliveries I bowled now. I said mainly outswing, but I do bowl a good slower ball that has claimed a lot of victims, ranging from Chris Broad downwards. I promised that I would bowl one for his benefit later on. That was the fateful ball. As I writhed in pain, I glanced up to that same balcony for some comfort from my old mate. There he was rocking from side to side again, with that silly great grin all over his face!

7 July

Gloucestershire 273 for 5 60 overs
Leicestershire 200 all out 47.2 overs: Lewis 53; Agnew absent hurt; Curran 3 for 31
Gloucestershire won by 73 runs

We were never in the match this morning. Briers played a loose shot in the day's first over, and after that it was downhill all the way. Willey, Gower and Whitaker soon followed. All the goals we set ourselves at the start of the season are vanishing one by one. The Benson and Hedges; we failed to qualify. We are bottom of the Refuge Assurance, and now we have failed to reach the quarter finals of the Nat-West. Disappointing does not describe it. We are not doing ourselves justice. The only thing that remains for us now is the Championship.

I could not hold a bat today. If we had needed only a handful of runs to win, then I would certainly have tried. But there was no point. The only good thing to come out of the match was Chris Lewis's batting. He showed everyone up, and demonstrated just what a good wicket it was by plundering the Gloucester bowlers, just as Curran had done to us yesterday. Peter Willey came and joined me on the balcony as I watched Lewis's onslaught.

"Just imagine if there had been someone else at the other end on 80 not out," he said. Quite right. We could have carried it off. Nothing much was said after the match. Nothing needed to be said. I don't think that anyone could believe just how badly we had been beaten.

I am out of the reckoning for Sunday's match at Trent Bridge. My hand is black and blue. I hope to make the trip to Old Trafford on Tuesday evening. Fielding will still be a problem, but as long as I can bowl and hold a bat, I will be there.

10 July

Refuge Assurance League

Nottinghamshire v Leicestershire

Match abandoned

Our first Sunday league points for a very long time. It looks as if we should pray for rain every week!

I was not at Trent Bridge to celebrate gaining two points. I went back to my roots. To the village of Ufford, near Stamford, where Ufford Park was in action against Oundle. Ufford Park was the first senior team I played for. I started there when I was a tearaway youngster, hurling the ball down as fast as I could. It was, and still is, cricket at its most rustic. The ground is a fenced off area in the middle of a huge cowfield. High oak trees enclose it, and there is a little stone pavilion tucked away just behind square leg, making the whole scene extremely attractive. I would have serious doubts as to whether George Ferris could fit his run up in on the field. There is only one problem: the resident herd of dairy cattle. During the course of almost every match the desperate cry goes up from the pavilion: "Watch out! Here they come."

The cows bear down on the players' cars, which are parked around the outside of the ground, and seem to have a particular penchant for the radio aerials. If unprotected, they are bitten off at the base. Play is abandoned while fielders and batsmen alike rush to save their vehicles, and the bravest shoo the cows, and solitary bull, towards the other side of the field.

My last match for The Park must have been in 1977, but nothing has changed. Virtually all the same players were there today. All, that is, except for Brian 'Baggy' Bagshaw, my new ball partner in those days. He has since hung up his size thirteens. Baggy would regularly bowl from one end all afternoon. And even though he had trundled away for Ufford for more years than he could remember, he happily relinquished his right to bowl downhill or with the wind when I came along. But, as senior statesman, he still always bowled the opening over of the innings!

There was Tez Rawlings the skipper and opening bat. He bustled up to me today, and asked if I could umpire as they were one short. Naturally I accepted. He was one of the league's most prolific run scorers and, until his knees gave way, he also bowled a useful medium pace. Ninety per cent of his runs came square on the off side, and I had a little chuckle when he dabbed one there off the back foot to get off the mark.

Being club captain meant that he was also responsible for providing the match ball. He would always save up the club's funds for when I played so he could splash out on a new ball. The times poor old Tez crouched at leg gully tearing his hair out as yet again I raced in and wasted it! Wicketkeeper Brian Hughes still talks of the times I bruised his chest as he tried to stop my wilder deliveries with wafer-thin gloves.

John Mason, Richard De Pear, farmer Peter Franks and his sons Willie and Mat, they were all there this afternoon. I didn't have to give any of them out in the course of the game, and it was a wonderful few hours spent in a level of cricket that has never altered. There is no mouthing on the pitch. No abusing the umpire when given out. Fielders applaud a good shot, and every batsman is clapped to the wicket. The only visible sign of modernisation at The Park is the appearance at each end of a very smart sightscreen. In my day I had the benefit of dark woods behind me. The batsman did not have a chance!

12 July

A dilemma. My hand is so sore that I'm not really fit enough to play. But I want to. I can bowl normally, just. Batting is still a real problem. I had a go in the nets this morning, and can block by using mainly my left hand. When a half volley came along though, it was extremely painful trying to hit it hard. I will just keep an end up when I play over the next three days, without trying anything adventurous.

As he promised, Andy Roberts came along to nets. His arrival coincided with my turn to bat which was most unfortunate. Of course he could not resist having a bowl at me. The first one was a rusty wide — it was his first delivery for four years! The second pitched on middle and off, bounced and left me resulting in the inevitable edge. I cursed loudly, bent down and picked up the ball. As I straightened up to throw it back to Fruits I caught sight of his face. Like a moonbeam it was. He was not very loose obviously, but that great action was still there. A slingy, side on delivery stride accompanied by a sharp intake of breath as he gathered himself, ready to propel the ball. That he was one of the greatest bowlers of all time is undisputed. Yes, he was bloody fast, one of the fastest ever. But he was also a great bowler. He could swing the ball, seam it, vary his pace, and bowl

117

from anywhere in the crease. A marvel to watch, and an honour to play with.

After my twenty minute nightmare I had a natter with Andy, and asked him if he had seen anything in my bowling which he thought I should work on. He said that I should be using the crease more. I bowl from very close to the stumps, my front foot landing on about middle and leg. It is good to get in that close without running on the wicket. It means that I have a great chance of getting an lbw because I am bowling dead straight, wicket to wicket. The ball is not angled down the leg side.

But Andy said: "The batsmen get used to the angle, especially if the ball is swinging. The more you swing the ball away from the bat, the wider you should try and get so the batter has to play at the ball because it's angled into him. If you can swing the ball away from wide of the crease, you will get heaps of wickets." I will try and work on that. Andy could bowl virtually any ball at will, including that outswinger from wide of the crease, and it often got a wicket.

I did not attempt fielding practice. My hand was very sore, and I did not want to make it worse. I will just have to hide on the boundary and hope the ball does not find me down there.

13 July

Britannic Assurance County Championship
Lancashire 304 for 8 dec: Fowler 75; Watkinson 85 not out; Such 4 for 81;
Agnew 0 for 53

Old Trafford. The name is synonymous with mizzly rain that never clears. Grey skies continually shroud the ground. And instead of blowing them away, the chill wind merely rushes in more of the dreary same. Apparantly you can see the Pennines from the visitors' dressing room once a year. On the days they are not visible it is because it is raining. On the day they are in sight, it is about to rain.

But the authorities at Old Trafford have decided to meet the elements head on, and with rather more success than Canute encountered when he attempted something similar. An enormous inflatable balloon has been installed in the middle of the ground, which, when fully unravelled and blown up, covers the entire square. When we arrived this morning to find it in all its glory, we half expected Richard Branson to appear from inside.

"It's like a giant condom," was one of the more outrageous suggestions. The fact remained though that after a night of near torrential rain, we started play only fifteen minutes late. Without its services, we would have been pushed to have played at all. As the monstrosity was being hauled in and stashed away in its covered trench, the new £8,000 water hog appeared and sucked up any remaining water in no time. Most countries have one

GREY DAY: No joy for me at Old Trafford.

Graham Morris

of these machines, but this particular model is definitely the Rolls Royce. Our's at Grace Road would be the equivalent of a middle of the range Skoda. Peter, the Lancashire groundsman, is very proud of his new toys, but he came in for some stick when the wicket appeared from below his new cover. It was completely brown, and had clearly been played on at least once before. I had heard Lancashire's captain, David Hughes, on the radio last night, complaining about the wicket we had played them on at Grace Road in the Benson and Hedges Cup earlier this season. "They'll find it rather different up here!" he promised. It certainly was. I do not mind people complaining about pitches if they are not producing wickets to suit themselves at the same time. But this one was clearly manufactured to assist their spinners. The first ball Peter Willey bowled today spun at least three inches.

For the seamers the track was a nightmare. The ball was like an old rag after twenty overs, and not one delivery deviated at all, all day. To make matters worse, Mike Watkinson and Jack Simmons launched a furious attack on the second new ball this evening.

I had my usual tussle with Graeme Fowler. He and I have been good mates since we played for England against the West Indies together in 1984. I joined the team for the final Test at The Oval, and Foxy had been bravely opening against them for the entire series. To make small talk before dinner on the eve of the match, I asked Foxy what it was like facing up to Marshall, Holding and Garner. Expecting him to say "terrifying" or something similar.

He simply said "great." And he meant it. That is Fowler. He loved the battle, win or lose.

We always have a good set-to along the same lines. One day will be his, another mine, but we both enjoy the confrontation. Today was definitely his, but not without a little foul play. As I was running in to bowl, and he was at the non striker's end, I was very aware of him staring at me. It was very off-putting. Then he took his helmet off, and really stared with his hands on his hips. After a couple more balls, I stopped on the way past him, and asked what he was finding so bloody interesting, or words to that effect.

"Did you know, Aggers, that your cheeks really bounce up and down when you run in to bowl?"

In the end I was running up sucking my cheeks in. All the time he would take his helmet off and look straight at me. I was finished.

14 July

Lancashire 304 for 8 declared: Such 4 for 81
Leicestershire 173 for 6 declared: Gower 96

A typical day's cricket at Old Trafford. On and off, on and off. The skies were dark all day, and there was a near-constant drizzle. David Gower found the conditions to his liking though. He played magnificently. He was furious when he holed out on the boundary just four short of his first century of the season. He needed that with the selection for the Headingley Test coming up this weekend. The Press say he may well lose his place, but with Chris Cowdrey now captain, I think he will stay. I know Cowdrey well, and he rates Gower extremely highly.

During one of the stoppages the *Cricketer's Who's Who* came out for the very popular time-killer, Silly Team Picking. There's a Fat XI, always captained by Mike Gatting, and featuring most of the Kent team; the Ugly XI, the Dickheads XI and so on. This time we assembled another group together under the collective banner of the Anorexic XI. It was not a bad team actually. Unfortunately I was included, and my new ball partner was Winston Davis with Neil Foster as first change. Heading the batsmen was Graeme Fowler. I told him about it in the pub later, and that Paul Allott was captain of the Truculent XI. Paul seemed quite pleased with that. He is a complete Jeckyl and Hyde character. On the field he is one of the most aggressive blokes around, and he loves to have a verbal go at the batsmen. Truculent describes him perfectly. Many of our young lads come off the field and swear blind that Walt is an unpleasant individual. They do not see him after the close of play though, when he is his true self; fun loving, and great company.

The game is nicely poised for a "fixed" declaration by Lancashire tomorrow, and a run chase for us. I would have thought 260 in 60 overs would be about right on this wicket. It should be a good contest.

15 July

Lancashire 304 for 8 and 119 for 2 dec: Mendis 51; Agnew 0 for 5
Leicestershire 173 for 6 and 133 for 9: Briers 37; Agnew 2
Match drawn

A really terrific finish, with our last man, Peter Such, having to survive the last two balls of the match to save the game. Not many of us in the dressing room actually watched those two deliveries, but Suchy groped forward with his pad and bat close together, and successfully negotiated them.

I had blocked for twelve overs with Whitticase. We had seen everything off that Lancashire could throw at us, including various comments such as "For God's sake get the lanky sod out before Bob Geldoff does a concert in aid of him!"

That was Fowler from first slip, still a little peeved to be included in my Anorexic XI. Spectators must wonder what goes on around the bat at tense moments. Well, there are flatulant noises released by the slips, as well as the odd silly comment, all designed to make the batsman have a little chuckle.

I was wearing my lucky trousers for my innings this afternoon. The only problem is that the crotch is ripped from dead centre down each leg for a length of about two inches each way. Normally I stick some white tape over the tear but today I forgot. Mike Watkinson was the first to spot it from his crouched position at silly point.

"Did you know you've ripped your trousers, Aggers?" (Pause while Flat Jack Simmons bowls a spinning off break which I successfully block.)

"Yes, I did Winker. I forgot to cover it up."

"Well from my position here, I can see the whole lot."

(High pitched voice from first slip again) 'Don't panic, Winker. One thing's for sure, not a lot'll drop out!"

That did it. I was laughing uncontrollably. Two balls later I was on my way. I actually walked for an lbw appeal. Jack bowled one which was short. I went back in front of my stumps to play the ball at about knee high. It shot straight along the floor, and hit the big toe on my right foot. I had no price. After all the grafting to be out like that! I sounded off at a few of the members as I made my way off the field and through the pavilion. I am not a bat thrower normally, but this afternoon The Raper flew across the dressing room accompanied by a foul oath. I was disgusted. Not with myself, not with anyone, but just with my luck to get a ball like that. Two runs were all I had to show for all that graft. Not even a not out to boost the average!

I saw Jack in the car park as I was packing my stuff into the boot of my car. "How the hell was I supposed to play that?" I asked.

"With a bloody shovel," Jack replied, making a kind of scooping action with both hands. At the end of the day it did not matter as we held on, but it would have been cruel if it had cost us the match.

Tomorrow is the West Indies match and I'm hoping to have the three days off. I have bowled an awful lot so far this year. People imagine you want to play and prove you should be in the Test team and to an extent that is true. Unfortunately we all know that the West Indian batters will be looking for as much practice as possible. We could be in the field for a very long time.

Kent were disciplined the other day for fielding a weakened side, contrary to the agreement between the TCCB and the touring teams. I see in tonight's paper we have named our full squad.

CHAPTER SEVEN

Fast and Furious

16 July

Tour Match

West Indies 150 for 4: Hooper 54 not out

I bowled flat out today. Faster than I have bowled at any other time this year, and probably last as well. My pace accounted for the wicket I took. I clean bowled Desmond Haynes after a razor sharp bouncer nearly decapitated him. I followed that with a slower ball, and then ripped his off stump out with his feet all over the place.

A large contingent of West Indian supporters enjoyed my spell. "Hey, Agnew! Peter May's watching you." I gestured that I could not see him anywhere. "He's over here, disguised in dreadlocks!"

I used to bowl that pace all the time, but I realised that I would only be physically able to play about half of the championship matches. I would strain muscles, and be sore and stiff, so that is why I settled for the shortened run up, and concentrated on swinging the ball. Today though, the ball did not swing, and so I really let go.

The rain came at about three o'clock and when we got off the field Andy Roberts was already in the dressing room brandishing a pack of cards!

Cowdrey's first Test team is being picked as I write. I wonder . . . Martin Johnson had me in his twelve in *The Independant* today. I was disappointed that there was no sign of a Selector at the match. I find that amazing. Apart from myself, there is Philip De Freitas and David Gower to watch, although Gower did not play in the end. I know that I made the Windies take note this morning when I was bowling. It would have been nice if a Selector had been there to observe. Gower did. He said that he really enjoyed watching it. I expect Neil Foster and Gladstone Small to get a Test recall. With Cowdrey as fourth seamer that would mean no place for me. Again.

17 July

West Indies 370 all out: Greenidge 75; Hooper 62; Dujon 51; Agnew 2 for 114
Leicestershire 33 for 4

Today we witnessed at first hand the terror of the West Indian fast bowling machine. Waiting in the dressing room, knowing that sooner or later the missiles which are currently being hurled at someone else's head will be directed at yours, is terrifying. You question your ability to get out of the way. "Will I see it clearly? Will I see it early enough? Will I react in time?" All batsmen, from the openers down to number eleven, feel exactly that way. There is none of the usual banter. Just a gasp or moan as another ball flashes past someone's head or smacks into already bruised ribs. It is easy to see why some of England's batsmen appear to have had enough of it.

There was quite a demand for protective gear today. I was padded up by the close and, apart from pads and gloves, I had a thigh guard on my left leg, another on my right thigh, a shin guard strapped to my left forearm, and a thick chest pad strapped over my heart. Plus of course, my helmet. These guys mean business and will let everyone have short pitched balls. It is a far cry from how it used to be, when bowlers *bowled* tailenders out. Tomorrow I will be their human target, just as the others in the team are. It is not a nice thought.

David Gower left before our innings started. That did not go down very well with the batsmen who had to go in and face the music. The majority of the team are not exactly delighted that Gower has pulled out anyway. He says he has nothing to gain by playing against them now. He has just finished a Test, and there is another starting next week.

I bowled a stack of overs today — 29 to be exact. So much for an easy three days. Lloyd Tennant turned up today to watch. He would have loved a game. So much for the theory that the members look forward to the tourist match more than any other in the season. Barely a couple of hundred turned up. There was a smaller crowd than for a run-of-the-mill Sunday league match.

It will be interesting to see whether Viv Richards enforces the follow on tomorrow if we are bowled out cheaply or just goes for more batting practice. The way things went today, if we avoid the follow on by scoring at least 220, it will be a miracle. If they want to bat again I think we should protest by not using our regular bowlers. I certainly do not want to bowl again. I am tired after my efforts today, and we have a vital week of cricket coming up.

Not selected for England. Disappointed, yes, because I feel that if I had been watched yesterday I might have been picked. Apparently it was between me, Pringle and Radford. Pringle won because of his batting.

I found a picture of me bowling Des Haynes in *The Sunday Express* this morning. I cut it out and slipped it in his kit bag before he arrived. It went down very well with their boys, and Desmond enjoyed it, but he did enquire if I remembered the Fifth Test at The Oval in 1984. Of course I did. Des scored a hundred and won them the match. He said he will put the picture in his scrap book. I offered to sign it for him. He grunted his disapproval!

18 July

West Indies 370
Leicestershire 90 all out: Agnew 8; Patterson 4 for 44; Benjamin 4 for 20
and 103 for 6

Match drawn

Laurie Potter today scored the best 16 not out I have ever seen. He batted for over two hours, did not give a chance, and took everything the West Indies's fast bowlers could throw at him. It was an innings of the highest courage and determination, and on another day it would be worth a century.

I got my innings over and done with before lunch. I batted for over half an hour, and fended a few off my nose. The most painful moment was when a Patrick Patterson full toss missed my pad and hit me on the left calf. I had shooting pains down my leg to my toes, and it was agony. That ball must have been travelling at at least 80 miles per hour, and did not hit the ground to slow it down. It thudded straight into my unprotected leg. Higgy found that hilarious. I was wearing more armour than a jousting knight, and then got pinned on the one bit that was not covered by foam or something similar.

Eventually Winston Benjamin got his revenge for my getting him out yesterday when I edged him to Viv Richards at first slip.

I enjoyed the contest generally. At the time it was hardly pleasant, but I did not give them my wicket. They did not have to work quite so hard to dispose of Suchy — an edge for two, then a straight ball cleaned him up — or Les, who won the toss with Suchy and therefore earned the right to go in last! In our score of 90, his was the only duck. Before going out to bat he ordered Peter Hepworth, today's twelfth man, to go and fetch him a cheese roll and a packet of smokey bacon crisps. "If my number's up I might as well go with a full stomach," he said. It was like watching a condemned man eating his last supper.

Then it was a case of trying to save the match, which we did, thanks to Potter and Whitticase, who stayed together for three quarters of an hour. I was due to bat next, but was spared another encounter with Patto. Instead of d.n.b. (did not bat) alongside our names on the second innings scorecard, Suchy reckoned that it should be Agnew, Such and Taylor,

SWEET SIXTEEN: Courage and class from Potter.   David Munden

d.n.f. — did not fend!

Unfortunately, very little positive emerged from this encounter with the strongest team in the world, except that Laurie showed his courage. The batsmen who were out of nick, are even more so now. I bowled 29 overs in their innings, and am now very stiff. Whitticase has aggravated his back strain, and Suchy has gone in the leg.

19 July

Day off. Spent the afternoon in the casualty department of Leicester Royal Infirmary. My hand is still very sore, and I find it very difficult gripping things. I struggled batting against the West Indies yesterday, and decided an X-ray was called for. It confirmed what I had suspected. My little finger is cracked between wrist and knuckle.

Fortunately there is no real treatment. I say fortunately, because it means I can still play cricket. It will just be very sore for the next six to eight weeks. I phoned Craig this evening to tell him the news, and I told him that I do not want anyone else to know. It would be too easy to use as an excuse if things go badly, and I certainly do not want the England Selectors to find out.

20 July

Britannic Assurance County Championship
Derbyshire 348 for 4: Barnett 200 not out

What an awful day! Mind you, Kim Barnett played well. He faced the first ball of the day, attacked everything, and blocked the last one to still be there tomorrow morning.

I cannot work out what has happened to the green seaming wickets we played on earlier this season. This one is easily the flattest pitch we have had at Grace Road all season. There is not a blade of grass on it, and it is very hard. Why have we now decided that our seamers cannot compete with Derby's? OK, they have Michael Holding in their team, but he is only one. The last result wicket we had here was the one against Kent, the second match of the year. We will not win the Championship if we keep playing on wickets like this one. Derby are fourth from the bottom of the table. They are no threat to us. We should have taken a gamble and taken them on. We desperately need a victory to stay in touch with the leaders.

I am completely knackered this evening. Jaded probably describes it better. I bowled another 21 overs today, and felt stiff all the time. The West Indies match really took it out of me. That was the first time that I have bowled consistently fast for a long time, and my body is not used to it. Unfortunately we are still in the field tomorrow morning. I cannot say that I am looking forward to it.

21 July

Derbyshire 429 for 6 dec.: Barnett 239 not out; Agnew 2 for 122
Leicestershire 254 for 3: Briers 125 not out; Boon 70

I remember the moment so clearly. The date was August 19, 1978, and Leicestershire were playing Lancashire at Grace Road. It was my first class debut. I ran in and bowled my fourth ball of the game, and shattered David Lloyd's stumps. He was my first victim. Today, ten years and 163 matches later, Bernie Maher drove me straight into Peter Willey's hands in the gully to become number five hundred. Nearly 4,000 overs delivered on first class grounds all over the world. It is a memorable landmark, and Paul Newman shook my hand as he made his way to the crease replacing Maher. "Five hundred up. Well done mate!" Two minutes later he was on his way back again; number 501.

Unfortunately I have a feeling that the wicket will end up the winner in the end. We should now avoid the follow-on without any problem, but Kim may be frightened to leave us anything to chase in the second innings.

Daffy is far from happy with life at the moment. He did not take a wicket this innings, and believes that we should be playing on a more helpful pitch to get a result. I think we will get that on Saturday against Essex. It looks very green at the moment. But if we do not bowl them out very cheaply we will be back to square one with our critics within the club. The pressure will be on. I am exhausted. 31 overs in this innings. Still five days to go until the next day off.

22 July

Derbyshire 429 for 6 and 125 for 5 dec: Agnew 1 for 36
Leicestershire 254 for 3 dec. and 183 for 8: Briers 60; Agnew 0 not out
Match drawn

Daffy has not been included in the team to face Essex tomorrow. At this stage nobody is sure what the official line is, but it appears that Nigel and the committee are dissatisfied with his recent efforts. He was very upset when he was dropped from the England team and he seems to have entered a bout of deep depression. Maybe a few days away from Grace Road will help get his mind right again. It is a great pity, because off the field he has been perfectly quiet. But he still is not on speaking terms with Willey or Potter and I am sure that is another reason for his being dropped.

Les comes back in. The wicket looks extremely green, but the comments have started already. "Cor, if you lot don't get them out before lunch on there you should retire" was one emanating from Will's corner this afternoon. I am saying nothing. I have seen green wickets at Grace Road do absolutely nothing. Fortunately Andy Roberts heard Will's comment, and echoed my thoughts.

We are still not playing very well. We never threatened to score the 300 we needed today, and in the end I was called upon to block two balls from Holding to stave off defeat. We should never have got ourselves in that position. Nigel played well again, but the rest of the batting crumbled as it has too often this year. Morale is low. There is the Daffy business, the same grumbles over the West Indies match, and our batting problems hanging over our heads. I am sure that a good win would help. I hope so. No one enjoys turning up to work when they are not enjoying it. At times like this, cricket becomes just a job.

23 July

Britannic Assurance County Championship
Leicestershire 226 for 6: Briers 118 not out
v Essex

Daffy was dropped for lack of effort during the Derbyshire match. Apparently he has pleaded guilty and he will not play again for at least a week. His excuses were that he was tired after playing for two years virtually non-stop, and that he was also disappointed after being dropped by England. I can understand the second one but he should have decided to get the bit between his teeth, and show the Selectors that they were wrong. Sulking only lets them question your character, and that can be held against you when a tour party is being selected. I cannot believe that he is tired. He has had to do very little work at Leicester so far this season. As for the last two years, he should consider himself fortunate to have been picked to tour Australia and then New Zealand. It is an honour that any county cricketer would give their right arm for. I can understand David Gower saying that he felt jaded after ten years of continuous cricket, but two years does not warrant that kind of sympathy.

Peter Willey is not a happy man either. He is suffering one of the leanest runs of his career, and today was run out backing up. Briers drove John Lever back down the pitch. Lever got a slight touch on the ball, which hit the wicket. Willey was inches out. It is the sort of freakish dismissal which always seems to get batters who are out of nick. I thought I would cheer Will up a bit. I was reading a magazine which was promoting schoolboy cricket, and pop star David Essex had written a few words of encouragement to the youngsters. "*Just remember that for every wide bowled or every duck scored, there is always another over to bowl or another innings to bat.*" I thought they

BRIERS' PATCH: Nigel runs into form.

David Munden

were excellent words, putting the whole game into perspective very simply. I read them aloud to Willey.

"Oh yeah, it's alright for him to say that," he snapped. "If his family ever gets hungry, all he has to do is stand up and sing a bloody Winter's Tale a couple of times and he's rolling in it again. What can I do when my poles keep getting blasted out?" I could not answer him. Singing in Will's case certainly would not solve the problem.

The start was delayed because of overnight rain, as was the Test at Headingley. Both teams crammed into our dressing room to watch the highlights of England versus The West Indies at the Oval in 1976. That was the match in which Holding took 14 wickets, and Viv Richards scored a magnificent double hundred. Both Peter Willey and Geoff Miller were present as we watched their efforts in that match, and there was plenty of leg-pulling all round. The only absentee was Andy Roberts, who turned up just too late.

Another excellent innings by Nigel has given us some respectability. The pitch is green, but has not done very much. I am glad that we have batted first.

24 July

Refuge Assurance League

Essex 133 all out: Lewis 4 for 13; Agnew 1 for 15
Leicestershire 137 for 2: Potter 66 not out
Leicestershire won by 8 wickets

Hooray! four points. Our first Sunday league win since the opening match of the season. It was a good all-round performance too, with the bowlers keeping things tight, and then the batters knocking off the total without alarms.

The difference today was that we kept taking wickets throughout their innings. It makes things so much easier. It is, in fact, quite hard to get people out on Sundays. There is very rarely a close catcher, and the only chance a bowler really has is for the batsman to have a wild slog, and get caught somewhere in the deep. Today we kept having the luck. Thin nicks were caught behind the wicket. Another day they would have gone wide of Whitticase for four. Chris Lewis bowled superbly. He is maturing as a cricketer. I have spent a lot of time fielding at mid off for him, and have talked to him throughout his bowling spells this season. He listens, and then decides if he will try what I suggest, or carry on with his line of thinking. That is what learning is all about. Listening, and then deciding for yourself. He frequently asks me questions about bowling when we are in the dressing room now. I am happy to talk and discuss things with him. If I can feel that I have somehow helped him, if only a tiny amount, I will be happy. He has enormous talent in every department.

Les received a communication from the Dutch Immigration Department yesterday, and brought it to the ground this morning. It is a very official-looking document written completely in Dutch. He showed it to me, and asked me what I thought.

"I haven't a clue," I said, handing it back.

"Well what about this then," he said, pointing to the last word of the letter. "Verpissen." They must reckon I was drunk on arrival at the airport. I've got them now 'cos I wasn't!"

Unfortunately Les's hopes were dashed by a member of the Hague Cricket Club, who happened to be visiting. It turns out that he has been found guilty of tampering with his passport and fined 200 guilders.

"Well what about this bit about being drunk?" implored Les. The interpreter looked at him quizzically, shrugged his shoulders, and left.

Andy Roberts also left today. It was sad seeing him go again. He has vowed to come back in four years' time. He reckons I will be ready for the knacker's yard by then. He is probably right too! When the Essex lads turned up this morning, I caught hold of David East and told him that we were giving a young seamer a run-out this afternoon, did he want to see him? I took Easty into our dressing room, and there was Andy on the phone. Easty's face was a picture! He sort of stammered a "Hello Andy," and then bolted for his dressing room spreading the news that Roberts was back!

25 July

Leicestershire 300 for 9 dec: Briers 119; Whitticase 50 not out; Agnew 18 and 42 for 1
Essex 200 for 3 dec: Border 65 not out; Prichard 71 not out; Agnew 2 for 43

I have an awful feeling that this game is going to disintegrate. George committed the ultimate crime of saying that he was fit to play on Saturday, and then breaking down after only two balls today. He is having problems with his left ankle, and needs time for it to clear up. He will not be able to bowl tomorrow. Nor will Chris Lewis. He has ripped a calf muscle. Les got hit on the right thigh while batting, which is showing all the signs of turning into a strain. We will have to see how he is in the morning. That leaves me and Willey to bowl.

Essex have spotted this, I think, by declaring early. They want us to set them 280 in 80 overs or so. I cannot see how we can leave anything without two or even three of our main bowlers. I know Essex though, or rather Keith Fletcher. He will throw up some rubbish bowling to make us look foolish by not declaring. Fletcher speaks his mind on occasions like that. He and I had a few words during my innings this morning. Ian Pont bowled

PRO AND CON: *Fletcher knows every trick.*

David Munden

Whitticase five bouncers in an over, and Fletcher kept saying "well bowled Ponty" and grinning all over his face. When the last one nearly hit Whitticase in the mouth, much to Fletcher's amusement, I lost my temper.

"It's bloody easy standing there laughing when you're fielding," I shouted. "Wait until it's your turn to bat."

He lost his temper too and we had a real slanging match. I was bowled in the next over, and, of course, he had a few things to say as I walked past. I simply said that I would see him in the middle later. He has not batted yet. He will, though, put enormous pressure on Nigel to declare. He is a vastly experienced and respected old pro, and if he is not happy with something, he usually gets his way.

26 July

Leicestershire 300 for 9 and 129 for 1: Briers 63 not out
Essex 200 for 3

Match drawn

Mercifully the heavens opened just before lunch and put everyone out of their agony. Nigel had broken the news to Fletcher that we could not set them a realistic target, and naturally the Essex boys were far from impressed. There were plenty of moans, and choruses of "You lot'll never win the Championship playing like this" which is true enough. But with George and Chris unable to bowl, we had no choice. Les's thigh was OK, but myself and Willey were the only other bowlers.

Three very welcome days off ahead. It has been a hard slog since the Windies match. There is an important burst coming up too, with Nottinghamshire at Worksop, leaders Kent at Canterbury and then Hampshire at Grace Road for four days. I cannot see George or Chris being fit for the first of those games. I wonder what they will do about Daffy.

29 July

There are those who say the being a professional cricketer means a glamorous life, and in the main I would agree. I have been fortunate. I have travelled much of the world, and having a name that is regularly in the public eye has its advantages. But today, the glamour is missing. We are in East Retford. Where? It appears to be a small market town just off the A1, some ten miles east of Worksop, another sparkling metropolis where we are due to meet Nottinghamshire in the Championship. Nigel, my roomie, has just walked in.

"If the wicket's anything like the town, I'm going to go in the hamstring in the morning!" he announced.

I have not seen Worksop yet, but certainly Retford is the sort of the place you drive through thinking: "I wonder what sort of people live here?"

The journey was uneventful, except Whitticase insisted on bringing his own cassette for the hi-fi system. The Goblins, The Blow Monkeys, The Wobblies — real trash. I will take revenge with some rather nice Bach I recorded the other day. I can see a change of navigator on the way.

30 July

Britannic Assurance County Championship
Leicestershire 257 for 9: De Freitas 113; Whitaker 61; Agnew 10
v Nottinghamshire

The Worksop ground was everything we imagined it would be. Half football pitch, half cricket ground, it lies at the back of the town centre bus station and alongside a canal. There is a local equivalent of the Sydney Hill opposite the canal — a run-down rough area at the back of the mobile chip shop. Gower suggested that people wanting to sit there should be armed with a complimentary scythe to slash back the knee-high grass and rambling brambles. Needless to say, no-one was seen venturing into that area all day!

The day was brightened considerably by a magnificent hundred by Daffy. It was the fastest of the season, beating Allan Lamb's effort by five balls. He destroyed Eddie Hemmings by peppering the area surrounding the canal before finally getting his range right, and landing one straight in the middle of the water to an accompanying cheer from the crowd. It was a great exhibition of big hitting, and got us out of trouble. I think he uses Ian Botham's script writers. Botham is the only other person I can think of who would come back from suspension and hit the fastest hundred of the season.

During a break for rain I indulged in a short game of cards with Franklyn Stephenson and Alan Whitehead, one of the umpires. Frankie has now taken over 85 wickets this season, and he is clearly delighted. He admitted to me that he felt that he was under enormous pressure at the start of the year, as he was filling in for two people: Hadlee and Rice. He has done admirably. Today he took six wickets, four with lightening fast yorkers. He is indeed a formidable opponent on the field, and more than useful at poker off it. And he is the only man I can think of who plays seven card stud wearing a cap!

STEPHENSON'S ROCKET: Frankie steams in.

David Munden

AGNEW'S EXPRESS: Four through the covers in reply.   David Munden

31 July

Refuge Assurance League
Leicestershire 130 all out (27 over match): Whitaker 51; Agnew 10; Emburey 3 for 15
Middlesex dnb

Match abandoned

There was a letter from the Test and County Cricket Board waiting for me at Grace Road this morning. It was from Alan Smith asking me if I am available for this winter's tour to India. The tour runs from the beginning of December until early February, and the pay is a basic £12,000. It did not say how many people were being sent these letters, but last year it was thirty, and I was not one of them. I filled it in immediately, saying that I would be available, and posted it this evening.

I tuned into Teletext this evening to see my name as one of the probable replacements for Graham Dilley in the Fifth Test, which starts on Thursday. Daffy, Thomas, and David Lawrence were the others. We will know tomorrow apparently. I cannot think it will be me. It would be rather ironic. I have had rather a lean time of things recently. That six-wicket haul at Gloucester seems ages ago. I do not think, either, that the replacement will play.

Our televised Sunday match was washed out. We finished our innings and then the heavens opened. I had lunch with Mike Gatting, which was an education. He started with soup, then he turned down the main course, which was roast beef. I asked him what was going on as he always enjoys his grub. He said that he was trying to lose weight. He ordered a massive portion of apple pie and custard, and then a plate full of custard on it's own. Some diet!

He has not changed at all, and I do feel very sorry for him. Things have not gone his way, but I think he is doing the right thing by having a winter off. I told him so, and he seemed pleased that someone agreed with his thinking. He is still as bubbly and entertaining as he ever was, and for that he deserves a lot of credit.

Simon Hughes was the latest bowler to fall foul of The Raper. He greeted me with a lively bouncer, but I replied with a hook and then an immaculate cover drive for four. Both shots made the highlights after the match was called off, and both teams sat and watched them together with plenty of leg-pulling and laughs.

SUCH RESPONSIBILITY: Peter's big day.   David Munden

1 August

Leicestershire 257 and 50 for 1
Nottinghamshire 367 for 8 dec: Randall 134; Agnew 6 for 117

A satisfying bowling performance, but my figures were ruined by Derek
Randall. The wicket was slow, so while there was nothing in it for me, it
was also far from ideal for playing shots on. Rags played superbly. Every
shot in the book came out, and he has put the match beyond our reach. We
must now bat well to save it. The pitch is taking spin, and because of their
lead, they will be able to have fielders around the bat for sharp chances. We
could not do that. Potter was hitting the batsmen's gloves twice an over,
but was hit into the river every over as well!

Although it was a warm and humid morning, the ball didn't swing at all
and after enjoying bowling flat out against the Windies I resorted to doing
that again today.

The morning belonged to Peter Such. He was not out over the weekend
for a princely six runs, and was thoroughly looking forward to continuing
his innings. Indeed, we wanted him and Les to bat well. It is the sort of
wicket on which every run is vital. This was the timetable of the biggest
morning of his career:

9.30: Suchy checked with Gower that he did not intend to declare. Gower confirmed that he wanted another ten or twenty runs if at all possible. Suchy was by now very nervous. He went through his usual warming up routine, but checked his watch constantly. He wanted to make sure he had enough time to relax before his innings.

10.15: Time for his cup of coffee upstairs.

10.30: After a nervous call of nature, it was time to strap on the protective padding. Two thigh pads, leg pads, protective box, arm protector and helmet. He was ready for action. After sitting quietly taking deep breaths, he asked me if I would throw him some balls to hit outside. Of course I agreed.

10.40: He was back in the pavilion talking tactics with Les.

10.55: The bell went and the Nottinghamshire players took the field. Off strode Les and Suchy accompanied by shouts of "good luck lads."

11.00: Franklyn Stephenson came running in for the first ball of the morning. It was a slow looseener. Suchy managed get some bat on it and set off for a quick single. He did not see that the ball had lobbed straight into short leg's hands.

11.01: Les shouted "No". He despairingly tried to make his ground. The fielder casually threw down the stumps, and Suchy was run out by a yard.

Then the hysterics started. Our whole team were writhing in the pavilion as everyone trooped off the field. Poor Suchy was distraught. I went outside as I was laughing uncontrollably, and managed to hear the conversation between two elderly men as they strolled in front of me. "Bloody waste of three overs that was," one moaned to the other. That is the stipulated number of overs lost between innings. Suchy's one ball had reduced the day's play by three overs. It was certainly one of the funniest incidents I have seen on a cricket field, and by this evening even Suchy was beginning to see the lighter side. He does so try and do his best with the bat.

After much speculation in the Press this morning, Daffy was called into the England squad for the final Test. His innings on Saturday must have swung it his way. I was disappointed. I still feel that I have done enough to earn a crack this year. I have now taken 66 wickets. 34 to go.

2 August

Leicestershire 257 and 200 for 7: Gower 72 not out; Agnew 9 not out
Nottinghamshire 367 for 8

Match drawn

A cloudburst at lunchtime delayed play for a couple of hours, and we escaped by the skin of our teeth, with a fine innings from Gower staving off defeat. Our batting is still extremely dicey and unless we improve dramatically we have no hope of finishing strongly in the Championship. We are now seventh, 63 points behind the leaders, Kent. We face them tomorrow.

I have already clocked up 560 miles since heading off for Worksop last Friday night. The trip this evening to Canterbury was tedious. After a hard day the last thing you feel like doing is getting in the car and driving for three hours. I met up with Whitaker and Boon in a Little Chef about thirty miles short of Canterbury, and we had a joke about the life we lead. People who think it is all glamour do not see what happens behind the scenes; the non-stop travelling and late nights, the quick snack in a roadside cafe. If we get the system right, with 16 four-day games, a lot of the travelling will be cut out. We in Leicester have it easy, too. Imagine how many miles the Yorkshire or Kent lads clock up every season.

3 August

Britannic Assurance County Championship

Kent 318 for 8: Pienaar 128

Despite the moans about the journey, Canterbury is my favourite trip of the season. We stay in The Woolpack, a delightful little pub in Chilham, where we are looked after magnificently. We have had some rare old end-of-season parties there, with all the normal games that go with them, but we are welcomed back every year.

The second attraction is the ground. Surrounded by tents and marquees, St Lawrence Park is a beautiful sight. Amazingly, there was a full house there today — on a Wednesday to watch a Championship match.

The crowd is so knowledgeable. Roy Pienaar was on 99, having blazed the ball to all parts, and I was bowling. I had to stop him reaching a hundred. Somehow I managed to bowl him a maiden over, and it got a tremendous ovation. The spectators appreciated the pressure I was under, and they enjoyed the contest. It makes such a difference from some of the partisan yokels we come across during our travels. The Kent crowd are a pleasure to perform to.

"Would you care for a Pimms old man?" replaces the "Oi! Has Daffy passed you the salt lately?" as conversation over the boundary rope. Very civilised.

I am not sure what the Mayor of Canterbury thinks about us though. Pienaar smashed one square off George, and the ball scorched to the boundary, hit the rope, and flew through the very narrow opening into His Worship's marquee. Our fearless third man fielder chased after it, but paused when he got near, expecting someone to emerge with the ball and chuck it back. There was no movement. Our man opened the flap and

KING PIEN: *Roy Pienaar put the pressure on.*

David Munden

went inside. There was the Mayor in full flow, delivering his after-luncheon speech. He was completely undeterred by the missile ricochetting around the four corners of his tent. That is more than you could say for his guests. One by one they emerged ashen-faced from beneath their tables, where they had dived for cover.

The wicket was exactly as I expected, slow and very low. It had been played on before, and will obviously turn later in the match. So far, though I have five for 59, and there are two wickets left. No complaints.

4 August

Kent 327 all out: Agnew 7 for 61
Leicestershire 247 all out: Gower 90; Agnew 0; Penn 5 for 68

My best bowling figures of the season, and the Press gave me a good write up this morning. It's interesting that my best performance should come when I'm bowling fast again. Bowling off a reduced run up for the past two seasons has improved my accuracy, and that showed today. I did an interview for the *News of the World* for this weekend along the lines of England's Invisable Man.

I batted number eight today, which is too high I think. We have a very long tail now. I got an awful nought, so did Les, and then I was called on to act as runner for Suchy, who damaged his ankle yesterday. It was the first time I have ever done it, and the stage was set for total chaos. We needed three more runs for a point from the remaining four balls. Such groped forward to the first three, and the fourth struck him on the pad. From my position at square leg, he looked to be an awfully long way down the wicket, and I thought that he would be spared. But up went the finger, and off we all trooped. Suchy was distraught. It seems often to be the case that lower order batters get fired out, and that certainly seemed to happen today. It happened to him last year at Derby to be the third victim in a hat-trick. That was a shocking decision, but because he was number eleven, and Peter Such, he was given out. Today he passed a large rubbish bin on the way back into the pavilion, and in disgust he threw his bat into it and stormed up the steps into the dressing room. The match is perfectly poised, and the wicket is now spinning square. We will have to bat well tomorrow if we are not to lose.

5 August

Kent 327 and 140 for 6 dec: Agnew 0 for 65
Leicestershire 247 and 203 for 7: Whitaker 48; Agnew 3; Harman 5 for 68
Match drawn

A very exciting match with our chase for 220 to win called off when I was out slogging, with 27 required off three overs. The pitch had exploded, turning at right angles, and was now looking more like the Canterbury by-pass. It was impossible to go straight out there and slog, and we could not afford to hand them the points on a plate. Again it was an excellent crowd, and they got their money's worth.

The journey back was appalling. I heard on Radio Kent that there were five-mile tailbacks approaching the Dartford Tunnel, so Geoff Blackburn, our scorer and Team navigator, decided that we would go through London and through the Blackwall Tunnel. He was in his element with two maps and an A to Z on his lap. It was after eleven when I got back, and I've clocked up 773 miles since last Friday evening when we struck off for Worksop.

CHAPTER EIGHT

Happy Endings

6 August

Britannic Assurance County Championship
Leicestershire 298 all out: Willey 98; Agnew 14
Hampshire 10 for 1

Sad to say that Grace Road was like a morgue today compared with Canterbury. There was very little atmosphere, and a very small crowd. Good old Dot was there in her red cap, doing her knitting in the seat she has made her own by the players gate. Goodness knows when last she missed a home match. But we need to find a couple of thousand more Dots from somewhere. Loyal supporters who will urge us on through thick and thin, not just when we are winning. Unfortunately our batting lacked any kind of inspiration, and only a Fred Carnoesque last wicket partnership between Such and Ferris gave our innings any kind of respectability. It ended in utter confusion with Such being run out off a no ball.

The wicket was very slow and flat. I asked Gower after play if we had now given up any hope of getting anywhere in the Championship, or if we were now trying a different angle of attack. Our battle plan had been to prepare wickets with pace and bounce. We have had two of those all season. This one was so slow that Willey bowled the sixth over of the innings. Gower did not appear too concerned. Having just witnessed Kent's pitches, which demonstrate why they are currently top of the table, I find this very disappointing. We will be very lucky to bowl Hampshire out twice on this.

I have pulled a few fibres in my left thigh, and so will probably miss tomorrow's Clash of the Giants in the Sunday league (they are third from bottom, and we are one below them). At least it will mean a bit of a rest

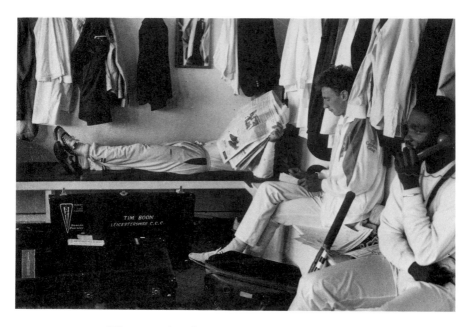

ELECTRIFYING: The atmosphere in the Leicester dressing room.   Graham Morris

after a very hectic week. Les might also miss out. He came up to me while we were batting this afternoon and said! "My knee's gone already. It's like a grape going off in there." Unusual symptoms, but nevertheless uncomfortable I am sure.

7 August

Refuge Assurance League

Hampshire 240 for 5
Leicestershire 177 for 7

Hampshire won by 63 runs

Another Sunday defeat — a good one to miss. I had a word with Gower after lunch and pulled out of the match. Spent the day sweltering in a garden chair instead. It was one of the hottest days I can remember in this country. I did spare the lads a thought, especially when the Hampshire score came up on Teletext. 32 extras seems rather a lot in 40 overs. They were experimenting with Benson behind the stumps because Whitticase was struggling with a pulled calf. I hope he did not have a nightmare.

146

8 August

Leicestershire 298 and 32 for 1
Hampshire 260 for 8 dec: James 77; Agnew 2 for 63

One of the most tedious day's cricket I can remember. Not helped by the slow pitch and accurate bowling, Hampshire struggled along at barely two runs per over until Bobby Parks and Raj Maru played a few shots at the end. Kevin James played well as night watchman, but the whole day was dreadful. County cricket at its worst.

Les's grape in his knee appears to have multiplied. He can now feel one in his left thigh. Gower, who fancies himself as something of a connoisseur, is extremely hopeful. "He's a walking vineyard," he said as Les was ruefuelly rubbing his aching limbs late this afternoon.

9 August

Leicestershire 298 and 212 for 4 dec: Whitaker 87 not out; Willey 56
Hampshire 260 for 8 dec and 233 for 9: Smith 68; Taylor 6 for 49; Agnew 3 for 79

Match Drawn

It is amazing how two such boring days can produce such an exciting finale. We had nine balls at their final pair, needing the one wicket to win. They had only just abandoned the chase for 251. It was a thrilling last couple of hours, and full credit must go to Hampshire for maintaining their charge.

We were all delighted for Les. He took six wickets in eleven overs, and kept us in the match. It was by far his best performance of the season, and he was really chuffed. It sounds as if there will be something of a celebration in the Taylor household this evening. As he took his fifth wicket he announced that he would be treating Our Sue to a "Chinky take — away."

Unfortunately he was brought smartly down to earth in the dressing room when he heard that he had to go and join the second team for the next three days at Kidderminster. He was distraught. He has played as much as the rest of us recently, if not more, and has earned a rest. And he has just recorded his best figures for some time. As I left, both Gower and Mike Turner were arranging a reprieve from Higgy.

George bowled at the speed of light this afternoon, and then went in the hamstring. It was frightening watching from mid off as he steamed in and peppered their lads with a lot of short stuff. It was a great effort on that wicket, and it was a tragedy when he suddenly pulled up with the injury. He will almost certainly miss Edgbaston at the weekend. Chris Lewis is still

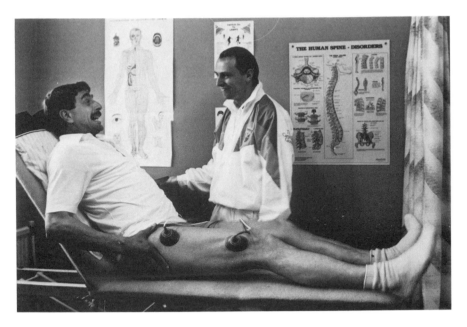

SWITCHED ON, LAID BACK: Two faces of Les.   Morris/Munden

out, so it will be me, Daffy and Les making up the pace attack.

Mark Nicholas scuttled up to me this morning. I have been previewing the major Cup ties in *Today* and Hampshire are in action against Worcestershire in the Nat-West semi-final tomorrow. "Aggers old chap, you will write us off again tomorrow won't you? You've done it twice now, and we've romped home." I assured him that I would.

12 August

There is a serious danger that I may not be fit for tomorrow's match against Warwickshire. I was batting in a benefit match at Kibworth this afternoon when a delivery hit me on the inside thigh. I knew as soon as it struck me that it had done the muscle. I left the match and went to see Craig for treatment. Will thought the whole thing was a sham to get out of today's match, but I was serious. The problem with these blows is that they turn into muscle strains as soon as you exercise. After the first treatment it was still very stiff but this evening after another session it is slightly easier. It will be sore in the morning according to Craig, but if I loosen up properly, he thinks I will be OK.

Lloyd Tennant stands by for me tomorrow. George is also going to give his hamstring a run out in the morning. He was unable to test it this morning because for some inexplicable reason the nets were not fit. The mood was really ugly when everyone turned up and were unable to have a knock or bowl. Will had driven all the way from Northampton. None of us had any reason to think that nets would not be prepared.

13 August

Britannic Assurance County Championship

Warwickshire 117 for 6

Good old Craig! My thigh passed a fitness test this morning. The wicket was unlike the recent pitches at Edgbaston. This one is slow, but seams a little. The other ones have, apparently, been like playing on a cobbled street. One ball is around your neck, the next from the same length raps you on the ankle.

This match has shown us for the first time what effect playing on dodgy wickets has on batsmen. The Warwickshire batters are shell-shocked. Whenever Daffy bowled a short ball today, they did not know whether to duck or stand up and play the ball. As a result they got hit by balls that were really innocuous. If this is the sign of things to come, then action must be taken now. These dangerous wickets must be outlawed before someone is seriously hurt, and the game becomes a complete lottery. Daffy bowled well between the showers today, but the most regular sight was Les

149

collecting the Queen of Spades during several hands of Sweaty Betty!

There was an interesting interlude at lunchtime. From the players' dining room we could see four scantily-clad females spreading a large tarpaulin over the outfield. Will, ever the optimist, said: "Useful, it's going to pee down again." But suddenly from the heavens appeared four parachutists. The idea was for them to land on the sheet, but the northerlies got a hold and the groundstaff were sent scuttling for cover as the sky divers were forced into an emergancy landing on the pitch. The object of all this was to entice more people into Edgbaston. It obviously worked. As soon as it was all over, and we trooped back on to the field, most of the meagre crowd was on its way home!

14 August

Refuge Assurance League

Leicestershire 109: Agnew 9
Warwickshire 110 for 5: Agnew 1 for 29

Easily our worst Sunday effort yet, and after some of our others this year, that is saying something. OK, the wicket was not the best, perhaps 150 would have been a decent score, but there was no way we could defend 110. I was at the crease with eight overs remaining, and with the match reduced to only 36 overs per side, that also took some doing. My first ball from Merrick hit me straight on the foot. Somehow I knew that it was going to hit me as soon as he bowled it, and I got the scream out before it actually crashed on to my big toe Everyone seemed to find my agony extremely amusing, and Tony thought he would try it again. This time he got the length wrong, and it turned out to be a lightening full toss which hit me straight in the stomach. That was enough. I got the white hankerchief out.

We dropped a couple of catches, so although we had taken early wickets, we were unable to keep the pressure on. Mercifully we are still one off the bottom. We have never finished bottom of the Sunday league. I hope this year will not be the first.

15 August

Warwickshire 181 all out: De Freitas 5 for 74; Taylor 4 for 19; Agnew 1 for 62 and 22 for 0
Leicestershire 206 all out: De Freitas 55; Agnew 0

There are two good things about Edgbaston. The A38 northbound, and Brenda. Brenda is one of the waitresses in the dining room. She always has the kettle on, and her speciality is milky coffee. From first thing in the morning until the last ball is bowled, she is there. She also makes a nifty

HIT MAN: Tony Merrick left his mark on me.   David Munden

cheese roll. The A38 northbound is great because it is the road out. Enough said.

Les bowled really well. He seems to have hit form. I eventually got a wicket — Norman Gifford, the number eleven.

My day was then completed by my second "first baller" of the season, and this one was authentic. Merrick bowled me a full ball outside the off stump. I went to prod it in to the covers somewhere, but I heard a snick. I did not feel anything on the bat though, and in that split second decided that I would not walk, but let Ray Julian, the umpire, decide. Out of the corner of my eye I saw a flash of white shoot past me. It was Merrick tearing towards the wicket keeper with his arms in the air, doing some sort of celebration dance. That was when I knew that perhaps I was struggling.

Ray gave a little nod of his head, and off I trudged. I thought that was a good effort of Julian's. He knew that I was unsure, and rather than stick his finger up in the air and make an incident of it, a little nod was all he had to do.

16 August

Warwickshire 181 and 173: Taylor 3 for 48; Agnew 3 for 65
Leicestershire 206 and 149 for 9: Briers 54; Agnew 5 not out
Leicestershire won by 1 wicket

Another thrilling finish. With two overs remaining, we needed six to win with three wickets left. I was batting with Whitaker, who had 36. Asif Din was bowling his occasional leg spin pretty well, but we were cruising. Then James tried to end it all off Din's first ball of that penultimate over, got an edge, and was brilliantly caught at slip. 1.5 overs to go. Six to win. Two wickets in hand. Les Taylor striding to the crease. We had a conference. "Nothing stupid, we'll do it in singles" was the plan. He failed to make any contact with the first four balls he faced, but got some bat on the last one, and we scampered two runs. Over. Four to win. Norman Gifford, the most experienced bowler playing the game today, to bowl.

Again Les and I had a chat. Again it was a singles-only policy. The first ball was straight and a good length. I pushed it straight back to Norman. The crowd went wild. The second was in the slot and I pushed it wide of long off. An easy two. The next ball was identical, but I hit it straighter. Too straight. I called Les back for the second, but Merrick was about to pick up the ball. I called Les to run because I knew that one fumble by the fielder or the man at the wickets would mean that we had won the game. I put my head down and ran towards my end. Suddenly there was a deafening roar, and I turned round to see Les setting off for the pavilion with the stumps scattered all over the place.

Three balls left and one run needed to win. Lloyd Tennant was the last man in. His eyes were sticking out like golf balls as he approached the pitch. "Back up Lloyd, and if you fancy a run, shout like hell," I said.

The fielders were all around the bat. It was like being a fly in a spider's web. The pressure was really on. The next ball was like the first of the over. Dead straight. I hit it back to Giff. Another roar from the hysterical crowd. The next was the same, but I tried to hit it to mid off. It went just to the left of the man fielding three yards from the bat. I set off, but then changed my mind. "No," I bellowed. Thankfully Lloyd was able to get back safely. Last ball, one run to win. "Run for anything," I shouted to Lloyd. At the worst we had tied the game, so we could afford to take a chance. No need. Giff bowled one on my leg stump which I gratefully nudged through midwicket. Game over. Victory.

It was not until I got half way back to the pavilion that I realised how much my legs were shaking. The pressure had got to me, and I was sweating buckets. Inside I apologised to Les, and we savoured our first victory for some time. We needed it too. There are only four matches left. We are now sixth in the table, but have played an extra game. There is not much time left to salvage something from this disappointing season.

19 August

Most of the morning papers had me in their team to face Sri Lanka. Again I had the feeling that I had a good chance. The main competition seemed to be Syd Lawrence. Dennis Coath, from Central TV, phoned and asked if I would do a live interview with him in their evening sports preview. But when I arrived he greeted me ashen-faced at the door. "I don't know how to say this mate, but you're not in. They've gone for Lawrence and Newport from Worcestershire, I'm really sorry." He was more upset than I was. True, I was disappointed. But I believe now that this particular group of Selectors do not think that I am Test class, and will not pick me. I had my chance four years ago. Perhaps I should have made a better go of it then.

Nets were cancelled again today because of the weather, and so was a session with Martin. We were going to discuss the final four matches, and try to find out why things this season have not gone as well as they should have done. We all know that. I suppose post mortems will be held after the season, but as things stand now we still do have the chance of finishing in the top three of the Championship. We are going to have to play really well to do that though. Tomorrow we meet Somerset at Hinckley, our only home match away from Leicester. Steven Waugh, their Aussie all rounder has gone back Down Under, which is a bonus.

It is past 9.30, and the phone is still ringing with people saying "bad luck". I am remaining philosophical about it all. I desperately want to get on the tour. I have four matches left to make a last impression.

VIC-TIM: But Marks got his revenge.

David Munden

20 August

Britannic Assurance County Championship

Somerset 158 for 9: Wyatt 57

It seems certain that Daffy will leave at the end of this season. He has been hinting as much for some time now, but today he seemed sure that The Committee will agree to his release.

Lancashire seem the favourites to sign him, but why on earth he wants to bowl at Old Trafford for the rest of his career I do not know. He and Neil Fairbrother are big mates, so I suppose that had some bearing on his decision. We will be losing a cricketer who can swing the course of a match in minutes. But by the same token he can be such a disruptive influence that the team should pull together better as a result. Clearly something either at, or about, Grace Road upsets him, and so it must be the best thing if he goes elsewhere.

If he is to be released then I can see no reason why he should carry on playing in the team this year. He does nothing but talk about leaving, and that is very unsettling. It is obvious that he cares little or nothing about Leicestershire's success now, and so should not be on the field with us.

I took five wickets this afternoon, which I suppose is the best possible response to yesterday's disappointment. All the lads expressed their sympathies today. It was good to feel their support.

Vic "Skid" Marks is far from happy. "Aggers, I thought Grace Road was the most awful ground in the country, now I know there is one worse!" To be fair, Hinckley is not that bad. It appears very amateur; the dressing rooms are tiny, and the wicket looks a bit rough. But the locals work really hard to keep their one match of the year, and this time have produced a very quick wicket. It is easily the fastest we have played on this year. To complete Victor's misery, I got him lbw second ball for nought. He is not relishing being on a pair at Hinckley.

21 August

Refuge Assurance League

Somerset 175 for 5 (37 overs): Agnew 2 for 34
Leicestershire 143 for 8 (29.5 overs): Agnew 19 not out
Leicestershire won on faster scoring rate

An amazing game — and not just because it was a Sunday league match which we happened to win. It was how we did it. After a couple of interruptions for rain, we had to get 143 from 30 overs to win. In our usual Sunday fashion we had slumped to 90 for seven with six overs left. I was leaving the dressing room on my way out to bat when I said to Les: "How do you reckon we should play it?"

"Just have a slog and get out", he said. "That's what I'm going to do."

I agreed, and met The Rat out in the middle. "Just push it about," he said. "It's only six an over."

Now you can see why he is an awful navigator. "It's more like tens," I said. "Let's have a welly."

So we did. He hit a few fours and then got out and we were 115 for eight with good old Lloyd Tennant on his way out again. 28 in two overs was the target. "We're knackered," I said to Lloyd. "Enjoy yourself." He did. So did I. The ball went everywhere. When I hit the last ball of the penultimate over for four, I felt that we now had a chance. The Grace Road faithful did not, though. They were busily filing out of the turnstiles.

Twelve were needed off the last over, bowled by Neil Mallender. Lloyd smashed the first two for four. He missed the third, and looked really upset. I went down the wicket and said: "Hey, We're on a hiding to nothing here. If you miss it, don't worry. No one is expecting us to win. Relax."

He got the next ball away to third man for a single. Two balls left, three to win. I decided that we should run the first ball, and if necessary slog the last. Roebuck, a cunning skipper, brought his deep fielders in five yards, cutting out the two, so there would be a lot of pressure on the last ball with more than a single needed. In came Mallender. The next split second is a blank, except the end result, which was the ball ricochetting off the boards at extra cover. We had done it. Another last over thriller, the second of the week, and the crowd went wild (or at least they would have done had they still been there!)

If only it had been a top of the table clash rather than a complete nothing game. At least it now means that we cannot finish bottom of the league.

22 August

Somerset 164 all out: Agnew 5 for 51 and 62 for 3
Leicestershire 233 all out: Whitticase 71; Potter 52; Agnew 0

It was announced officially today that Daffy is leaving us. The Press have descended on Hinckley, and already the phone is ringing with offers from interested counties. Mike Turner said that because of Daffy's approach and attitude it is better that he and the club part company. Apparently Turner had told him that if he did not give 100 per cent or if the situation was intolerable he would release him. Turner said that he couldn't see the situation improving next year and so decided to release De Freitas. Daffy responded by saying that he had not enjoyed his cricket at Leicester for the past two years, and that he always felt he was being picked on. Everyone, myself included, feels that it is a great shame that a cricketer of Daffy's ability should be going to play for someone else. He is a match winner, and we would like to have had him winning games for us, rather than another

LEAVE 'EM TO ME: George getting mean again.   David Munden

team. Shame it did not work.

The question now is whether or not he plays for the rest of the season. The majority of the team feel that he should not, and that is also my belief. Firstly, it is clear that his loyalties now lie elsewhere, and Leicestershire's fortunes are unimportant to him. Secondly the players likely to replace him next season must take the opportunity of gaining valuable experience now. People like Lloyd Tennant and Peter Such should play. I am sure that Mike Turner also feels that way, it is a question of how Gower sees it.

I am on a pair at Hinckley. It serves me right. And guess who got me out? Victor Marks, second ball, caught at short leg off one which turned and bounced. He gave me one of his toothy chuckles as I walked past him towards the pavilion. He did not say anything. He did not need to!

Fortunately Whitticase and Potter played superbly after we had been in real strife again. I was padded up at lunchtime at 96 for five, but did not get in until a couple of overs before tea. It is quite exhausting sitting in the dressing room waiting to go in. I watch every ball, others do not. Gower sits and does the *Telegraph* or *Independent* crossword. Others chainsmoke or chatter nervously. Some simply pace the floor. All a personal way of dealing with nerves.

I got back into the dressing room, sat down and started to take off my pads. George was already at the crease, and there was an enormous appeal from the middle as he received his first ball. He survived, and then there was the sound of stampeding elephants thundering up the stairs towards the dressing room. The door burst open and there was Les, panting, his face as red as a beetroot.

"You're not really out, are you?" he puffed. "It's tea."

"Of course I'm out," I snapped. "Look at the scoreboard." Then I realised what the problem was. Les had been on the phone at the back of the pavilion, and could not see the game. He was now next in. He was wearing a T-shirt and had no padding on. There had already been a hysterical appeal against George, who is a reasonable batter, but a Number Ten after all.

The rule is that the incoming batsman has two minutes to get on to the field. There was no way that Les would make it if George got out now. He would have to face a ball without pads on. I have never seen Les move so quickly. There were chest pads and arm guards everywhere as he struggled with the straps and buckles, but he made it. Sweating profusely, he staggered to a chair to sit down, only to see the umpires removing the bails for tea. "Bloody typical," he moaned.

23 August

Somerset 164 and 170 all out: Marks 50; Ferris 4 for 36; Agnew 2 for 34
Leicestershire 233 and 103 for 3
Leicestershire won by 7 wickets

"Winter's on the way," Les announced first thing in the dressing room today. "My shallots were drooping this morning. That's the first sign of a frost you know."

No one dared argue with him. I do not think any of us would know a shallot if we trod on one, let alone a frost-bitten specimen. Weather forecasting is Les's domain out here in Hinckley. It is his home territory.

Nip in the air or not, it was a good victory today which has lifted us to sixth in the table. Victor avoided his pair, and then played well for his fifty. But their total was a poor effort, and we knocked off the runs comfortably.

Daffy has played his last first class match for Leicestershire. It was decided today that he would not be travelling to Glamorgan tomorrow, but would see out his days with us in the second team. That will have virtually put paid to his hopes for going to India, but we have to rebuild our team. Gower said a formal goodbye to him in the dressing room:

"Thanks for what you achieved while you were with us Daffy. When it was good it was great."

That summed it up well. A few of us went along for a farewell drink with him that evening. After he left, James Whitaker and I had a long discussion on how we would like to see Leicestershire pick itself up. We agreed on one point; this season has been a great disappointment. We have only three matches left to salvage some pride.

158

CHAPTER NINE

Welsh Wails

25 August

Leicestershire 301 for 6: Whitaker 126; Potter 66; Agnew 14 not out
v Glamorgan

"What the hell are we doing here? Even all the trees seem dead." That was one of the comments flying around the dressing room on our arrival at Castell-nedd; that is Neath to non-Welsh speakers. I can think of more attractive cricket grounds; Hull, Faisalabad, and Ahmedabhad to name but three. It is part of the rugby ground, very open. The biting cross wind did not drop lower than gale force all day. Mind you, the hospitality is splendid with enormous cream teas served with a friendly smile. The wicket, unfortunately, is as dead as the atmosphere.

Dickie Bird is on duty here, so I made sure I checked on his condition first thing this morning. Apparently he is now 100 per cent fit. The first over of the match was delivered from his end, and no sooner had he got things under way than a rogue dog appeared on the field from the fine leg area. It proceeded slowly towards the wicket, ran right past a frantically waving Dickie, and seemed to disappear off the pitch at long on. Relieved, Dickie gestured to the bowler to get on with the game. As he was half-way through his run up, Nigel pulled away from his batting stance, and pointed up the wicket. There was the dog, cocking it's leg against the sightscreen behind the bowler's arm! That was too much for Dickie, who charged after the animal, which simply jogged back the way it came, across the wicket and off at fine leg.

Our batting was as flimsy as ever, but there were some agonising dismissals. Nigel was out hit wicket as he tried to stop the ball rolling back on to his stumps. Unfortunately in so doing his bat hit the wicket. Dickie confirmed later that the ball would have missed anyway! Gower was then

159

caught behind down the leg side off their spinner. An awful death. When he came back into the dressing room he erected a makeshift gibbet, and attempted to hang himself with his own benefit tie. After several attempts he gave up because he could not kick the chair away from under him.

James and Laurie then played really well on the desperately slow track and gave us some sort of respectability. The Rat and I were padded up for over three hours, and in the end were taking it in turns to decide who would go in next. Unfortunately it was my turn as James hit a catch, and in I went.

I did not middle one ball. Everything went through the slips. In the end it was embarrassing. Umpire Shepherd was standing there again like John Wayne about to draw his Colt 45 because I reminded him of the lbw at Gloucester and the whole thing was becoming hilarious. Potts then nicked a wide one to the keeper, and as he set off to the pavilion Dickie shouted at him: "It's a four-day game lad!" That was too much for Potts, who really hates getting out. He stormed into the pavillion with his bat flailing.

"What's up with him, Jonathan?" Dickie asked innocently.

"I think it may have had something to do with that comment of yours Harold," I suggested. But Dickie was right. We had not reprogrammed ourselves, and Potts and I should really have been playing for tomorrow. Willy, Leicestershire's answer to Michael Fish, informs me that the forecast is appalling. Rain, rain and more rain. We really do not need it.

26 August

Britannic Assurance County Championship

Leicestershire 314 all out: Agnew 21
Glamorgan 11 for 2: Agnew 0 for 2

The day dawned brightly enough, and I was really excited. Not out over night, with the chance of dipping my bread on a flat pitch against a weakened attack. I got to the ground, got changed and had a hit on the outfield. It was then that someone spotted it. An enormous fog-like cloud had completely blacked out one of the hills on the far side of the ground. It made the whole place seem eerie, like a horror movie. "If that lot moves into the valley, we've had it boyo!" announced one local cheerfully. After much messing about getting the covers on and eventually off the field, we got underway, and collapsed. The ball swung all over the place, and we lost four wickets for 13 runs. I was the first to go, driving loosely. I could really have kicked myself. I had thrown my chance away.

George steamed in and got two quick wickets, then sure enough the fog descended and that was that. The ground seemed to be swallowed up by this cold wet cloud. No more play, but plenty of Sweaty Betty. There are

145 points available every hand, and all four of us now have approximately ten thousand points each. That is forty thousand points, divided by 145, equals apprixmately 292 hands of cards since the start of the season. Will reckons that last year we had 15,000 points each, so on that basis, this summer has been drier. It's the weatherman in him.

27 August

No play. Rain

Plenty of cards, but otherwise no game. It has been raining all day. Apparently Llanelli, venue for tomorrow's Sunday League match, is underwater. They only have plastic sheets as covers there. It seems tomorrow will be equally boring.

28 August

Refuge Assurance League

Glamorgan 77 for 7: Agnew 2 for 13
Leicestershire 80 for 2
Leicestershire won by 8 wickets

The most unpleasant day's cricket I have ever known. We were the objects of continuous abuse, with David Gower being the one to cop the most. We arrived at the ground expecting the worst, and sure enough the pitch was virtually underwater. Under normal circumstances the match would have been called off there and then. But this situation was far from normal.

Glamorgan had a mathematical chance of reaching the play-offs for the Refuge Assurance Cup, and so they needed to play. If they beat us and Gloucestershire lost to Essex, they would qualify. So they hung about to see if there could be a ten overs slog at five thirty. The main problem was that the ground was full of spectators who had been told at the gates and on the phone that there would definitely be play. Dickie blew up at one of the officials who was happily telling people phoning in that play would start at two o'clock. The wicket was soaking wet and the umpires felt under enormous pressure.

Meanwhile it rained again, but no one went home. The beer tent and bars were doing a roaring trade, and by four, the mood of the natives was definitely ugly. There were drunken Welshmen everywhere, and when the Glamorgan team went out on to the field in whites there was uproar because the crowd then assumed that it was us who did not want to play. The umpires had another inspection, and decided that we should have a thirteen overs per side match.

We got changed and went on to the field to loosen up. That was when the abuse really started with filthy language and insults being thrown in our direction. Suddenly the match changed from being a farcical slog in unfit conditions to a war. Our backs were up. We really wanted to win. We got together in a kind of huddle in the middle of the pitch and got ourselves fired up. Outnumbered and threatened, the only way was to show what we could do. And we did.

Our fielding was brilliant, and we bowled really tightly. Every boundary for the home team was greeted with a tumultuous roar. When we took a wicket, there was stony silence. 78 to win. We had to do it. We got into the dressing room, which was the size of a prison cell. All around us were beer-swilling yobs hurling insults and pushing and shoving. None of us watched the match. There was only a tiny slit for a window. We just waited for the roar to signal a wicket.

A fight broke out outside our room. We saw the brawlers being led away. There were only two policemen on duty in our area, and no stewards on our door. Our toilets were invaded by the yobs. The atmosphere was frightening. The amazing thing was that when we won, the crowd had gone in ten minutes. We had been worried about the reception we might get, and thought our cars might be vandalised. But when we poked our heads out of the pavilion door, there was no-one to be seen.

We later had a couple of drinks in the hotel bar, and the major topic of conversation was the incredible team spirit we had shown. If only it could be like that all the time.

29 August

Match abandoned

The game was called off at nine o'clock when Dickie and Shep failed to reach the pitch. They could not get there for fear of being bogged. The whole place was underwater. The groundsman had scattered sand everywhere to soak up the puddles, but it had made it worse.

"It's like low tide at Skeggy beach, Jonathan," moaned Dickie.

It is so disappointing. We badly needed to win this match, and we were in a good position. Personally it has made it very hard for me to get 100 wickets. I am on 89 with only two games left. If there is any more rain, I have had it.

30 August

Britannic Assurance County Championship
Leicestershire 314 for 7: Gower 146; Potter 85; Agnew 4 not out
v Nottinghamshire

Our last match at Grace Road this season. The wicket is green, but looks as if it will be another typically deceptive Leicester wicket. None of us were upset when John Birch won the toss and stuck us in.

David Gower opened the innings. He thought that this would take some pressure off Boony, who has struggled recently, and there was a buzz of excitement as Gower strode to the wicket. An hour later he had scored 47 as the team floundered on 55 for two, and even more remarkably at lunch he was on 85 with the total a dismal 112 for four. It was vintage Gower. Boundaries flowed effortlessly from his bat, with the ball disappearing to all parts of the ground. He seems to have that split second longer to see the ball than other top batsmen. Today against a hostile Franklyn Stephenson, the difference showed. Time and again he smashed him square for four on the off side.

We see an awful lot of cricket during the summer and when we are batting only a couple of players actually watch the cricket out in the middle. The others chat or read newspapers in the dressing room. Les sleeps. But today everyone watched David in action. It was compulsive viewing. Laurie Potter also played really well, and was strangled out 15 short of his ton.

We got the impression that the Notts boys do not fancy the wicket or George Ferris at all. There has been a lot of talk about having Friday off, and their record here recently has not been good. Winston Benjamin has rolled them out a couple of times. Will has noticed that Randall in particular appears rather apprehensive, and told Rags that George is after him. Another 30 or 40 runs tomorrow will be very useful.

Umpire Kevin Lyons will remember his trip to Leicester for some time. He had his car stolen last night, and all his umpring gear was in it. His white coat, black trousers, white shoes, the lot. He took to the middle today in a borrowed coat, which was enormous, and the trousers of a pin-striped suit. When I saw him first thing he was hoping that his colleague for the match would be about his size — around five foot eight, so he could borrow a spare pair of trousers. Of course one of the tallest umpires on the circuit, Roy Palmer, was down to stand with him, hence the suit trousers. His car has still not been found.

163

GOWER AND GRACE: *The skipper in sparkling form.*

David Munden

31 August

Leicestershire 332 for 9 dec: Agnew 15 not out; Stephenson 4 for 107
Nottinghamshire 118 for 8

Rain washed out much of today's play, but it couldn't hide a great team performance. What we suspected about their batters proved true this afternoon. George bowled really quickly, with a lot of short stuff. He sent Randall's off stump flying out of the ground which made Will's day. Unfortunately rain is forecast for the whole of tomorrow.

We batted on this afternoon, hoping to get to 350 odd. The Rat and I put a few on, but then Stephenson bowled him and George in successive deliveries. Big Frankie turned to me and said "Only Les to come," with a massive grin on his face. He clearly fancied getting his hat-trick. But his smile disappeared immediately because Gower declared. He wanted a few overs at them before tea. Les had his leg pulled unmercifully. We reckoned that he paid Gower off.

2 September

No play. Rain

Deep depression. More Sweaty Betty. The Rat is now through the 12,000 barrier.

3 September

Leicestershire 332 for 9
Nottinghamshire 133 all out; Ferris 5 for 49, and 258 for 7: Randall 90,
Agnew 3 for 59

Match drawn

We got close, but again we have to count ourselves as victims of the weather. We were always going to struggle to take thirteen wickets in a day. In the end we took ten. Randall batted superbly — a similar innings to the one he played at Worksop. "I hope you get your hundred wickets Aggers," he said to me as he walked in to bat. "I'm afraid you won't get me though!" He was right. I never looked like getting him out.

So that is the end of our season at home. At the close we sat in the dressing room and shared a couple of bottles of champagne. They were the results of the Player of the Month award, which Whitaker won, and I was awarded the Player of the Year.

The time has flown by again. March 23, the day we reported back for training, seems only a few weeks ago. In fact it is nearly five and a half months. We have nets next Thursday and then there is only one game left, in a week's time at Chelmsford.

The tour party is very much on my mind. It is announced next Thursday, and I am more and more convinced that my name will not be among the sixteen. My face does not seem to fit. If it did I am sure I would have played against Sri Lanka. Dickie Bird feels the same way too. He said at Neath: "I'll do what I can, Jonathan, because I think you deserve to go lad, but I don't think you will."

It is satisfying from a purely personal point of view to have taken wickets again this season. Whether I go to India or not, I believe that I have justified my decision to stay in cricket, and again that is important. I now need seven wickets for the ton. Seven in one match. The pressure is on.

7 September

I have not been picked for the winter tour. I am so depressed. What more can I do to get it through to those blokes that I can bowl? At the start of the year Peter May said that they would be picking players in form. I would have thought that 93 wickets so far this summer suggests that I am in reasonable nick. Kevin Cooper at Nottingham is the only Englishman who has taken more.

The suggestion that I can only take wickets at Grace Road? My best performances of the year have all been away from home — seven for 61 at Canterbury, a six at Worksop and a six at Gloucester.

Fitness suspect? Well, like last summer, I have not missed a Championship match all season. I have even played for half the year with a cracked bone in my hand.

The last time I had any contact was when Micky Stewart phoned me to tell me that I was very close to being picked for the First Test this summer. "Bad luck. Keep going mate," he said. No-one has a right to play for England. I know that. But what have I done wrong since that phone call? How can I have been so close then, and nowhere near three months later? All I have done is take more wickets.

When other players come up to me and ask what I have done to upset the selectors it really hits me. So far two fast bowlers who I am competing with to get into the England team have asked that. One of them has got on the tour.

I spent today with Pat Murphy commentating on the Refuge Assurance semi-final between Worcestershire and Middlesex. I found it quite terrifying. It is one thing to broadcast to Leicester, but this was national on Radio Two. It is a lot harder than I thought. I can empathise with the Radio Three Test Match Special lot. They must be real pros.

Tomorrow we go to Chelmsford, and the baby is due the day after.

Gower will make sure that we have a twelfth man down there in case I am called away.

8 September

The tour party was the major talking point during nets this morning. The more we talked, the more it became clear that many of the players asked about their availability for India had received a phone call from Micky Stewart. I still had not. In the end I decided that I would take the bull by the horns and phone him myself. I got through to his secretary, but he was unavailable. She promised me that he would call me later in the afternoon. James Whitaker paid up the £10 bet we had about me going on tour. The lads were most sympathetic.

Sure enough at about half past four the phone rang at home and it was Micky Stewart. I started by asking him what I had done wrong since May when he had last got in touch with me and told me that I was very close to being in the team for the First Test against the West Indies.

"You've done absolutely nothing wrong, Aggy," he replied. "And I can tell you that you were only a fag paper away from playing in the Fifth Test at The Oval, and likewise against Sri Lanka at Lord's. You just missed out."

I said: "Well if I just missed getting in a party of twelve, how come a couple of weeks later I can't get in a squad of sixteen?"

He started to explain why I had not been picked, but he was really talking about why the likes of Newport and Lawrence had been chosen.

I said: "Micky, it doesn't concern me at all why others have been picked. What I want to know is why it wasn't me. And what I really want to know is whether my omission was for reasons other than cricket."

"I can assure you Aggy that it was purely on cricketing grounds."

I mentioned the history between myself and Fred Titmus, that I felt that Fred did not rate me at The Oval when he was coach, and that he had not changed his mind.

"That's not true, Aggy. In fact Fred was the first to raise your name at the meeting on Tuesday."

"So you're telling me then that the reasons I was not picked to go on the tour were purely on cricketing grounds and nothing else."

"Yes. No-one can take away what you have achieved over the last couple of years. It is a great effort, but you have just missed out."

"Well if that is the case," I said, "I can accept it. You and the Selectors have made your choice, and it is your job to do that. I'm bloody upset at missing out, especially after being told that all selections were being made on form. What I can tell you Micky is that I'll be back again next year with another hundred wickets, and then you'll have to pick me."

And that is where we left it.

CHAPTER TEN

Les the Legend

9 September

Britannic Assurance County Championship
Essex 362 for 6: Stephenson 99; Waugh 86; Prichard 59

Although the score would suggest otherwise, this was a really good effort. The pitch is really flat. It is slow in pace and nothing has moved off the straight all day, except when Peter Willey turned a couple late on. It is the best wicket we have seen all season. Add the hot weather to that, and the score could well have been a lot higher.

Everyone got stuck in and worked hard. The spirit was excellent. It is so easy on days like today for things to drift. You can resign yourself to the fact that they are going to score millions and you are going to be in the field for hours. We dropped a couple of catches, but there was no shouting or histrionics. People grafted for each other.

I did not take a wicket, so am still on 93. The way the match is going, I cannot see myself getting to the century mark now. Tomorrow will probably see Peter Willey go for his first hundred in county cricket. It is incredible to think that he has never had it done to him before. His figures overnight stand at four for 98, so he has only two runs to go. He bowled well today, and although he obviously got hit as much as anyone else, he remained calm and seemed to enjoy the challenge. In fact he retained his humour well. When another of his deliveries got smashed out of the ground for six, he examined the replacement ball and said "This one's no good. I'll have to have another over and see if I can lose it!"

It is great fun playing at Chelmsford. There was an excellent crowd and they like to see cricketers enjoying themselves. Essex has a record of having a terrific team spirit, with past characters such as Ray East, John Lever and

Keith Pont, all of whom were known as practical jokers. There is a particularly friendly ice cream lady, who took pity on Les and me when we were sweating away on the boundary edge. She came around the rope and presented us each with a raspberry split which was gratefully accepted. The other lads in the middle were not too amused though as they watched us sucking away!

Neil Foster and Derek Pringle have both grown grotesque beards, neither of which have more than ten hairs to the square inch. Pringle has grown his to stop him cutting his throat after missing out on the tour! He reckons that Foster's is made of iron filings, and that if one was to hold a magnet a foot away from Fozzie's face, his beard would fly out.

Late in the day the news came through that the tour was likely to be cancelled after eight visa applications had been rejected. Naturally with Graham Gooch being a central figure in the affair, the media descended on Chelmsford. Cameras of all shapes and sizes were pointed at the players' balcony for most of the afternoon. A TV crew got the picture they wanted; Pringle had made his own banner and draped it over the edge of the balcony. It read:

I don't care. I wasn't going!

The black/white split that everyone has been dreading for the last few years is now a serious possibility. The thought is too worrying for words.

No word yet from Bev. The baby is due today. I'm all set for a midnight dash to Leicester.

10 September

Essex 592 for 8 dec: Hussein 162 not out; East 68; Willey 4 for 163; Agnew 0 for 122
Leicestershire 218 for 4: Gower 143 not out

I have never been on the receiving end of such a massive score before. It was a nightmare. The ball just kept on disappearing to the boundary. We were put out of our misery shortly after lunch when Gooch declared, but the Essex bowlers found that the pitch was still as flat, and they suffered unmercifully at the hands of Gower. He agrees that he has never played better, and has never hit so many boundaries. Everyone was on the balcony to watch him in action this afternoon. It was sheer poetry.

But the fact remains that we need a total of 453 just to make them bat again. It will be a minor miracle if we do that. They can afford to have men catching all the time, as the pressure is on us. When we eventually got off the pitch, the bowling figures were read out, agonisingly slowly. The extras contained 25 no balls. "Just think lads," said Gower. "We'd have kept Essex down to only 567 without them!"

We think we have discovered one of the reasons for Essex's success over

'PLEASE ....?': No relief ... and no wicket.

Graham Morris

NOW, WATCH: Les demonstrates the Shilton Drive.

David Munden

the past decade — George's orange juice. George is the dressing room attendant at Chelmsford, and is responsible for maintaining a constant supply of liquid refreshment in the visitors' dressing room. This consists of pure orange juice, and after two days of high temperatures, the effect of too much pure fruit juice is having a dire effect on the team. We are doing well to have eleven men on the park at the same time, and those that are on the pitch are often to be seen crouching in the outfield with a pained expression! I noted that the machine in the home dressing room serves lemon and lime squash.

11 September

Essex 592 for 8
Leicestershire 268 all out : Gower 172; Boon 63 not out; Agnew 2; Childs 6 for 92,
and 241 all out: Taylor 60; Agnew 4; Childs 5 for 88
Essex won by an innings and 83 runs

That is the end of our season, one day earlier than planned. The result was quite predictable after their massive first innings score, but it was still bitterly disappointing to finish with such a thrashing.

The scoreline above is not a mis-print: Les really did score 60. It was the first half century of his career, and the Essex faithful left Chelmsford clutching their completed scorecards knowing that in years to come they would be the envy of the cricketing world.

"Yes, son, I was there," they will proudly boast when little Johnny stumbles across the match in a back number of *Wisden* one day. And because the innings was so memorable from beginning to end, they will have no difficulty recalling the drama in the minutest detail.

‘ *Leicester were in deep trouble. Terrible trouble. They had no chance. They were hundreds behind Essex with one man left. Leslie Brian Taylor his name was. A giant of a man with shoulders like one of those American footballers you see on Channel Four, and a thick black moustache.*

As he walked out to bat there was silence all over the ground. You could hear a pin drop. He stood at the wicket and stared the bowler straight in the eye. Dead mean he was. He hadn't given up hope. He pulled on his gloves. But one of his team mates had filled the right one with orange peel and he couldn't get it on. Yard after yard he pulled out. Talk about laugh.

Then he was ready. He didn't block a single ball. Six after six he smashed right out of the ground. One bounced all the way down Chelmsford High Street and killed old Mr Samuel's pet ferret.

He only missed one. As he played the shot he pulled a muscle in his leg and jumped three feet into the air. The language was terrible. I'll never forget it.

The best bit was when he got his fifty. He didn't know he had done it. I remember the Essex wicketkeeper, a lad called East, tapping Taylor on the shoulder and pointing to the scoreboard. Dead chuffed he was. He held his bat right up high saluting the enormous crowd. He had never done that before, so he didn't realise he was holding the bat the wrong way up.

I'm afraid he got out in the end. A brilliant catch. Taylor hit this ball like a missile. People in the crowd started screaming, diving for cover. Suddenly from nowhere this boy dived five yards and caught it one-handed. Broke all his fingers it did.

And that was that. Essex had saved the match. Taylor so nearly won it for Leicester. He was a national hero of course. Finished up doing adverts for breakfast cereal on TV.

Les was knackered when he came off, but as he slumped into his chair he muttered: "See, it's an easy pitch when you get your head down!"

I popped my head around their dressing room door to say well done, and then remembered that Geoff Miller had announced his retirement earlier in the season.

"Good luck, mate," I said. "Enjoy it!"

'Hadn't you heard?" said John Childs. "He's changed his mind. He's playing on next year."

"That's right," Miller added. "Mind you, now Les has hit me for six, I think I'll definitely pack up."

Peter Willey decided that my trusty left boot had seen better days. On close examination I could see that he was right. After two seasons and nearly 1,500 overs the sole was warped and the inside was shredded. Will had thought of the perfect way to dispose of it. He would launch it into the River Chelmer which runs at the back of the pavilion. With a small and somewhat bemused crowd gathered at the foot of the pavilion steps, Willey slung the boot into the river. It was last seen floating perfectly upright under the bridge on it's way to the North Sea.

As I left the dressing room, the talk was mainly of the approaching winter, and how people would pass the time. Whitaker is thinking of going abroad. Les is working on his benefit. Willey is working in Northampton. George is returning to Antigua next week. Briers is going back to Reading and his teaching job at a prep school, Whitticase is running the indoor nets at Grace Road.

Soon after saying farewell I was in my car ploughing back up the M 11. The very last leg of our ten thousand mile trip which started in March when we set off for the Isle of Wight, and took in 17 first class grounds all over the country.

Every season passes quickly, but this one in particular seems to have flown by. It has been a disappointing six months. We set out firmly believing that we could clean up in all the major competitions, yet we ended up with nothing. We didn't even get close. Obviously we over-estimated our ability. Those two early crushing wins in the Championship gave a false impression of how good we were.

A lack of runs, particularly in the one-day matches, was a factor. All our batsmen hit form at some stage of the summer but we rarely had two firing together. If only David Gower had found his end-of-season touch in May. Nigel Briers enjoyed one of the best years of his career, and James Whitaker played some memorable knocks. Tim Boon's broken arm meant a cruel end to his highly promising start to the season.

Laurie Potter played some vital innings going in at number six, but I think the player who made the biggest advance was Phil Whitticase. His wicket-keeping was spectacular, especially standing back. By the middle of the season his batting form had returned, and he made some valuable runs. He is also a chirpy character who keeps the team going on the field. Just do not let him get his hands on your road map!

Peter Willey had a disappointing season by his own very high standards. He bowled well when he got on a wicket which suited him, and a man half his age would have been proud of his fielding in the gully. He has vowed revenge on all the county bowlers for next year.

Of course the De Freitas business had an unsettling effect on everyone. At the start of the season I believed that he had got himself sorted out. But it is clear that there are two very definite, and very different sides to his character. He can be a happy-go-lucky individual, who enjoys a laugh and a joke as much as the next man. He cares intensely about the team's performance, and loves nothing more than charging in and taking wickets. Then something will suddenly trigger off a dramatic change. He becomes moody and insular. His natural aggression on the field then becomes directed at his own team rather than at the batsmen. A dropped catch will provoke a torrent of abuse. What we all failed to discover was what it was that caused those dramatic changes. Not even his best mate, Whitticase, could figure it out. Perhaps if we had, he would still be a Leicestershire player now. We all honestly wished him well when he left, but at the same time hoped that he would realise sooner or later that he will have to knuckle down. Lancashire is a hard school. No nonsense there. He is such a talented cricketer with such a natural flair for the game that he should be an England regular by now. If he wants to be completely honest with himself, maybe he should ask himself why he is not.

When Daffy was firing our bowling attack looked lethal. George Ferris bowled as quickly as anyone at times, and never gave anything less than 100 per cent. He is deeply worried though about what next summer holds with the return of Winston Benjamin. I think one of the highlights of this season was seeing George's face when he received his county cap.

175

SHARP WHIT: James played some memorable knocks.   David Munden

Chris Lewis came on in leaps and bounds, but was over-bowled at crucial stages of the season. It is difficult to believe that he is only 20. A fast bowler of that age must be looked after. He matured as a batsman, and proved that he is one of the most talented young cricketers in the country.

Good old Les showed that there is no substitute for a bit of experience. He battled away defying injuries as diverse as a septic mole under his armpit to haemorrhoids. And, as ever, his presence was excellent for team spirit. If ever someone deserved a bumper benefit, it is Les Taylor next year.

Peter Such suffered from a lack of opportunity. Rarely did we find a wicket which suited him, and too often for his liking he found himself sitting the match out as twelfth man. His is a classic victim of the decline of the old-fashioned spinner. He cannot bat, and is hardly a Colin Bland in the field, so is therefore considered a luxury in the team when Peter Willey could bowl his overs for him. The fact remains that he is a class spinner, and it would be a shame to lose him.

That just leaves me. The only thing that has changed since March is that I have decided to stay in the game. I failed to get back into the England side, but I remain convinced that the path I eventually took was the right one. I will miss broadcasting this winter, but I now have the challenge of selling cricket to teachers and schoolchildren, and I am looking forward to it.

Even in my wildest dreams I did not think that I would be in the position of taking one hundred wickets again. It at least showed that last year was not a flash in the pan, and although I only finished on 93, I think it proved a point.

As for the England situation, Robin Jackman's words in The Tavern at The Oval still hold true I have to make it impossible for them not to pick me.

It might seem strange, but as the miles roll by on this final journey, I am already thinking ahead to next summer, to once again doing battle with that helmeted fellow standing 22 yards away with a bat in his hand. Pitting my wits against his.

But more important to me is the handshake afterwards and the time when friend and foe alike get together to relate stories and incidents that have happened along the way. Maintaining the friendships which have been forged over the years. That is what cricket is all about.

Statistics

FINAL TABLE

	P	W	L	D	Bt	Bl	Pts
Worcs (9)	22	10	3	9	55	75	290
Kent (14)	22	10	5	7	57	72	289
Essex (12)	22	9	5	8	61	69	282
Surrey (4)	22	7	5	10	57	72	241
Notts (1)	22	8	8	6	34	71	229
Warwicks (15)	22	6	8	8	48	74	218
Middlesex (16)	22	7	3	12	49	54	215
Leics (3)	22	6	3	13	56	63	215
Lancashire (2)	22	6	7	9	41	67	212
Gloucs (10)	22	6	7	9	52	59	207
Somerset (11)	22	5	6	11	48	65	201
Northants (7)	22	5	7	10	48	71	199
Yorkshire (8)	22	4	6	12	48	65	177
Derbyshire (6)	22	4	3	15	53	54	171
Hampshire (5)	22	4	6	12	33	69	166
Sussex (17)	22	3	11	8	37	65	150
Glamorgan (13)	22	1	8	13	42	53	111

● *Nottinghamshire total includes 12pts for win in one-innings match. Somerset and Lancashire totals include 8pts for drawn matches in which scores finished level.*

1987 positions in brackets

Refuge Assurance League

FINAL TABLE

	P	W	L	T	NR	Pts
Worcestershire (1)	16	12	3	0	1	50
Gloucestershire (3)	16	10	4	0	2	44
Lancashire (9)	16	10	4	0	2	44
Middlesex (10)	16	9	3	0	4	44
Surrey (7)	16	8	5	1	2	38
Glamorgan (14)	16	8	5	1	2	38
Kent (6)	16	7	6	0	3	34
Yorkshire (12)	16	7	7	0	2	32
Hampshire (7)	16	7	8	0	1	30
Warwickshire (8)	16	6	8	0	2	28
Essex (14)	16	6	8	1	1	28
Somerset (4)	16	6	9	0	1	26
Derbyshire (5)	16	5	8	1	2	26
Northants (10)	16	4	9	0	3	22
Sussex (14)	16	4	9	2	1	22
Leicestershire (12)	**16**	**4**	**9**	**0**	**3**	**22**
Notts (2)	16	3	11	0	2	16

1987 positions in brackets

First class averages
(Leicestershire C.C.C matches only)

BATTING

	Innings	Not out	Highest	Total runs	Average
D. I. Gower	30	3	172	1107	41
J. J. Whitaker	39	5	145	1223	35.97
N. E. Briers	41	9	125*	1335	34.23
L. Potter	34	7	107	885	32.78
P. A. J. De Freitas	20	1	113	481	25.32
P. Willey	40	1	130	978	25.08
R. A. Cobb	20	2	65	432	24
T. J. Boon	23	1	131	505	22.95
P. Hepworth	6	–	51	132	22
P. Whitticase	32	10	71	469	21.32
C. C. Lewis	23	4	40	400	21.05
J. P. Agnew	29	8	38	271	12.90
G. J. F. Ferris	20	8	36	139	11.58
L. B. Taylor	16	6	60	111	11.1
J. Benson	1	–	3	3	3
L. Tennant	2	1	3	3	3
P. M. Such	6	2	6	9	2.25

*not out

BOWLING

	Overs	Maidens	Runs	Wickets	Analysis
P. A. J. De Freitas	465.3	111	1302	61	21.34
G. J. F. Ferris	452.1	81	1380	62	22.26
J. P. Agnew	747.5	159	2253	90	25.03
L. B. Taylor	324.3	70	967	35	27.63
C. C. Lewis	391.4	83	1210	42	28.81
P. M. Such	123.2	22	340	10	34
L. Potter	98.4	26	293	8	36.63
P. Willey	341	106	803	19	42.26

Also bowled: L. Tennant: 7-2-19-1

Catches
J. J. Whitaker 17; L. Potter, D. I. Gower and N. E. Briers 14; P. Willey 12; R. A. Cobb 10; C. C. Lewis 9; T. J. Boon 8; P. A. J. De Freitas 6; L. B. Taylor 4; J. P. Agnew 2; G. J. F. Ferris. Sub 3. (J. Benson, C. C. Lewis, P. Hepworth 1 each)

Wicket Keeping
P. Whitticase	Caught 69	Stumped 4
M. A. Garnham	Caught 2	
C. C. Lewis	Caught 1	

Refuge Assurance League averages

BATTING

	Innings	Not out	Highest	Total runs	Average
N. E. Briers	14	2	54	373	31.08
L. Potter	14	2	66*	366	30.5
J. Benson	5	1	42*	119	29.75
L. Tennant	4	3	17*	28	28
P. Hepworth	3	–	38	69	23
C. C. Lewis	6	2	40	92	23
J. J. Whitaker	13	2	51	238	21.64
G. J. F. Ferris	5	4	13*	21	21
J. P. Agnew	9	4	19*	87	17.4
P. Willey	11	–	43	168	15.27
T. J. Boon	3	–	22	44	14.67
D. I. Gower	11	1	50	124	12.4
P. A. J. De Freitas	8	–	37	74	9.25
P. Whitticase	7	1	21	51	8.5
L. B. Taylor	5	2	5*	10	3.33
M. A. Garnham	1	–	0	0	0

* not out

183

BOWLING

	Overs	Maidens	Runs	Wickets	Analysis
G. J. F. Ferris	64.4	4	266	15	17.73
J. P. Agnew	80.1	6	303	14	21.64
L. B. Taylor	74.5	–	379	15	25.27
P. M. Such	7	–	53	2	26.5
C. C. Lewis	58.4	1	249	8	31.13
L. Tennant	42	3	170	5	34
P. Willey	78	4	316	7	45.14
P. A. J. De Freitas	56.5	3	233	5	46.6
L. Potter	8	–	54	1	54

Catches
P. Willey 5; L. B. Taylor, C. C. Lewis, P. A. J. De Freitas, N. E. Briers, L. Tennant 2 each;
J. P. Agnew, G. J. F. Ferris, P. M. Such, T. J. Boon, J. J. Whitaker 1 each.

Wicket Keeping
P. Whitticase   Caught 17   Stumped 1
Benson   Caught 1